METAMORPHOSIS

METAMORPHOSIS

A MEMOIR OF TRANSFORMATION

MY APPROACH TO FACING TRANSITIONS IN LIFE

Megan Silletti O'Block

For information about ordering books, please contact
Diamonds Dishes, info@diamondsdishes.com.

Design by Robert Parsons / Seven Elm
Cover illustration by Melinda Beck / The i Spot
Interior illustrations by Steve Sanford
Back cover photograph by Megan Witt
Printed by The Studley Press, Dalton, MA

ISBN 978-0-578-53047-5

"Twenty years from now you will be more disappointed by the things that you didn't do than by the ones you did do. So throw off the bowlines. Sail away from the safe harbor. Catch the trade winds in your sails. Explore. Dream. Discover."

—

Mark Twain

This book is dedicated to my brother Johnnie who died very suddenly last year.

Johnnie was a high school English teacher and was planning to retire at the end of this school year. We were going to write a memoir together. I was putting the finishing touches on this book when I received the fatal phone call. Just before we unplugged his life support systems, I kissed him on his forehead and whispered in his ear, "Please, Johnnie, visit me often. I'm going to miss you so much." I cry every morning and every night when I say my prayers. I know he would be so proud of me for finishing this book.

I love you, Johnnie
Forever and Always

10/10/53—11/11/18

CONTENTS

Prologue		12
01.	**Spirituality**	20
02.	**Meditation**	44
03.	**Energy**	64
	Tai Chi	67
	Qigong	71
	Tarot Cards	75
	Feng Shui	77
	Chakras	80
	Reiki	85
	Crystals	88
04.	**Numerology**	92
	Astrological Chart	98
	Akashic Records	100
	Past Lives	102
05.	**Ayurveda**	108
	Recipes	120
06.	**Rituals**	136
	Epilogue	172
	Gratitude	180
	About the Author	186

PROLOGUE

I decided to write this book primarily for closure. I have learned so much these past few years and have journaled throughout, and I felt I needed to bring it all together in one place.

On this journey, I have learned that we can't carry with us regrets from the past or fears of the future; we need to live, as much as humanly possible and as hard as it may be, in the moment. I decided early on to take the bull by the horns and approach this new life with courage, confidence, and faith. Although at times it has been difficult, it has never been dull. Far from it. It's been more like a roller coaster, exciting with its slow ascents and anticipation of the inevitable drops, uncomfortable with its scary, neck-breaking twists and turns, and plenty of gasping along the way!

2016 was the beginning of this wild ride. At fifty-six years old, my marriage of thirty-three years was on auto-pilot and menopause was over. I had a long, hard conversation with God, and I gave him hell. Women have to go through childbirth, raise children, feel the emptiness in their hearts when those children leave our nest, and just when we are ready to circle back to ourselves, we go through menopause! Since I was pissed at God and I am competitive to a fault, I decided I would take on menopause like no other woman in history. I mean, I was going to do it even better than Eve herself! So, what did I do? I changed everything about my life!

In the next three years, my marriage officially ended and I moved from the northeast corner of America to Southern California. I left behind friends, changed what I ate, how I cooked, where I shopped, and what I wore. I gave away lots of my designer clothes and mostly live in jeans and sneakers now. I went from playing competitive tennis four days a week to yoga on the beach and sunrise hikes in the canyons. I went from a big house in the suburbs to a third-floor walk-up apartment with rented furniture. I joke with friends and say if I could rent the pillow-

INSPIRATION | JON KABAT-ZINN

"ASK YOURSELF FROM TIME TO TIME, 'AM I AWAKE NOW?'"

cases I would! I left behind fancy cars and leased a jeep. I wear less makeup, dyed my hair lighter, and even changed my part. I used to wake up to super strong Italian roast coffee, now I drink green tea. I wish I could say I stopped drinking alcohol, but in fact I drink more. Turns out there are a lot of divorcées out there who are happy to meet for a martini!

But I digress, I want to go back to why I'm writing this book. During all of the changes I made, I discovered meditation and other avenues that have helped me to have a healthier mind, body, and spirit, and that's what I truly want to share with you. Divorce is hard, but if I've learned anything, and believe me, I've learned more in the last three years than I did in the last twenty, it is that although change is difficult for everyone, going through it is when you learn and grow the most. If you look at nature, there are changes happening every second, and nature just adapts and accepts them. Humans, however, resist change.

Right when I was finding my feet in my new life in California, one of my lifelong rocks, my big brother Johnnie, died. So, my new life has been far from the Leslie Gore song *Sunshine, Lollipops and Rainbows*. When Johnnie died last fall, I was devastated by grief, and I'm still navigating that profound loss every day of my life. But as I move forward, I'm constantly reminded—by friends, by God, by strangers in line at the farmers' market—of the power of laughter to help heal the deepest wounds.

Frankly, I am very proud of myself. Although these last three years were the most difficult in my lifetime, I got through them. I didn't go around pain, over it, or under it—I'm getting *through it* with hard work. I want to share with you the fruits of my labor so you, too, can feel the pride of accomplishment on your own journey. My goal in sharing this is that something in it, even one small thing, resonates for you. If I can empower others, then I'll be happy.

Every time I tried something new, I would find a person who would suggest something else. There isn't anything that was suggested to me that I didn't explore. Some of it you might find too freaky. That's completely fine, don't do those parts. But if there is anything in this book that I really want you to at least try, it is meditation and journaling. The Tai Chi, Qigong, Reiki, and Numerology are things I personally loved learning, but I know they're not for everyone. The raw science behind the benefits of meditation, however, is not something to dismiss. Now, do I see lavender light and float peacefully throughout my entire day when I do it? Nope. But I am not giving up on it, either.

I am a visual learner, so I will be sharing a lot of visuals throughout this book. One image that kept coming to me during this transformation was a butterfly and the stages of metamorphosis. I was going through stages, from darkness to light, and eventually acquired wings to fly.

INSPIRATION | DOLLY PARTON

"IF YOU WANT TO SEE THE RAINBOW, YOU NEED TO PUT UP WITH THE RAIN."

I have also included a playlist as I did in my last book, *Heart to Table.* In every chapter of our lives, we listen to different types of music. I found what I've listened to during this journey is so very different. The playlists included at the end of each chapter start slow, and just like my journey, build and end with life-affirming and uplifting music. I also added some healthy new recipes for you to try in the section on Ayurveda. I just love experimenting in my kitchen with new herbs and foods from different cultures, and combining that love with my newfound interests in mindful, meditative living has been an absolute joy.

I want you, the reader, to know that we all have to make the best of this life, and we can, no matter what we're up against. There will always be moments of joy and moments of pain. As the saying goes, "Pain is inevitable, suffering is optional." So, please hop in, buckle up, and join me. We're in for one hell of a ride!

THE KEY | EXPLORE SYMBOLS

Throughout the book I offer suggestions of things you can try, read, research, listen to, watch, and explore more if you're so inclined. Here is a key to the symbols that you'll encounter:

Mobile Apps   Movies   Videos

Books   Podcasts   Websites

Instagram   TED Talks   YouTube

Spotify. Check out my custom playlists on Spotify: meganoblock.

01.

"WE ARE NOT HUMAN BEINGS HAVING A SPIRITUAL EXPERIENCE. WE ARE SPIRITUAL BEINGS HAVING A HUMAN EXPERIENCE."

SPIRITUALITY

I've always considered myself a spiritual person. I love entering a church and smelling the scent of candles and polished wood. It brings me tremendous solace just being in a physical space of worship, and when it's time to sing, I'm so happy to join in.

Whenever I have moved, the first thing I've done is look for a welcoming, comfortable church. Growing up Catholic, my mother marched all six children down the aisle every Sunday like the duck family in Robert McCloskey's book *Make Way for Ducklings*. I can see my mother now, beautifully dressed with her head held high; she was always so proud of her children and their good manners.

I stopped being Catholic after my mother stopped being Catholic. I'll never forget the day my little sister came out to my mother. By then, my mother had left my father and moved to California. She was incredibly happy in her one-bedroom apartment. She called and, at first, I thought she was laughing, but later I realized she was crying. You see, I had never, ever heard my mother cry. We were not a crying family. As a kid playing in the streets of New Jersey in the early sixties, if we fell and got a nasty gravel skinning from skidding into first base, which was Mrs. Bacci's curb, we didn't cry. We got up and toughed it out and got back in the game. My father, smoking a cigarette on the porch, would call out in his thick New Jersey accent, "You're fine babe. Get up, walk it off."

I remember saying to my mother, "Why are you crying, Mom, we all knew she was gay." I'll never forget my mother's response. "I know," she said, "but I'm afraid of how people will treat her." Such a quint-essential maternal response. No matter how old our children are, we always have this natural instinct

INSPIRATION | VINCE LOMBARDI

"IT'S NOT WHETHER YOU GET KNOCKED DOWN, IT'S WHETHER YOU GET UP."

to protect them. We see it everywhere throughout the animal kingdom. It's a little better now, but this was in the early '90s, pre-Ellen Degeneres coming out on prime-time television and before *Will & Grace* helped shift culture to a more accepting stance towards LGBTQ+ people. My mother was what I would call a staunch Catholic. She went to church every single Sunday. I can see her twisting her wedding ring around the whole hour. Now, years later, it's sad for me to think of that because I know she was probably praying for her marriage to improve, but at the time I was too young to understand how miserable she was. She said to me that day, "If they can't accept my kid, I'll never put another god damn penny in that basket." And she didn't. While she may have been a staunch Catholic, she was also a woman of her word. She never went back.

So, after years of taking my three sons to church every Sunday just like my mother had taken me and my siblings, when they grew up and left my nest I explored other religions. One day, while out driving, I passed this beautiful stone church that looked like something you would see in the English country-side. Outside, it had a huge rainbow banner with the

EXPLORE

#spirituality

#spiritual.thoughts

#spiritualitydaily

words, "Everyone Welcome." I went the next Sunday and found a wonderful community. I learned quickly that the reverend, Jeff, who had been a Catholic priest before becoming Episcopalian, was nothing like the Catholic priests I was used to. As a matter of fact, we called him by his first name, and that is something you would never even think of doing to a Catholic priest. Hell, in my Catholic grammar school, if a priest even visited your classroom you were trained to immediately get down on your knees.

Jeff's love for his parishioners was palpable. One Sunday shortly after I began attending this parish, a young couple was preparing to move to Chicago. Jeff asked them to step up to the altar and then asked the congregation to come close and touch each other's shoulders so that everyone was physically connected to the couple. This was also early on in my metaphysical exploratory journey when I was learning about energy and how everything and everyone has energy, even the trees and flowers that we pass on our walks. He placed his hands on the couple's heads, and with tears sliding down his cheeks and a

27

choked voice, he wished them love and guidance as they ventured to a new city. He told them how much the church would miss them. It was such a powerful and touching experience; I was hooked. Soon after, when my sons were home for Christmas, I asked them to join me at a service, and having them there with me somehow made my transition away from Catholicism seem official.

Interestingly, it was Jeff I reached out to for advice when I was truly struggling with my decision about whether or not to stay married. His response, after I described the previous ten years of my marriage, still brings tears to my eyes. It was exactly what anyone

EXPLORE

Broken Open
Elizabeth Lesser

Heal Thyself
Louise Hay

Make Way
for Ducklings
Robert McCloskey

Siddhartha
Hermann Hesse

The Holy Bible

Oh, the Places
You'll Go!
Dr. Seuss

The Power of Now
Eckhart Tolle

The Universe
Has Your Back
Gabrielle Bernstein

The Book of Joy
The Dalai Lama
and Desmond Tutu

You Can Heal Your
Heart: Finding Peace
After a Breakup,
Divorce, or Death
Louise Hay and
David Kessler

The Path Made Clear
Oprah Winfrey

EXPLORE

The Profound
Journey of Compassion
ted.com/talks/swami_
dayananda_saraswati

We Can Be Buddhas
ted.com/talks/bob_
thurman_says_we_can_
be_buddhas

who is struggling with a really tough decision would want to hear and likely very different from what I would have heard from a Catholic priest. He said, with such kindness in his voice, that it sounded like I had done everything in my power to try to make it work. He went on to say that I was a child of God and like any parent, he wanted me to be happy. That's the kind of church I want to attend, one full of love and compassion. When you think about it, it's exactly what Jesus was trying his damndest to preach!

For the last thirty-three years, I've had the unique opportunity to spend summers in a beautiful community in The Hamptons. After changing from Catholic to Episcopalian, I began to attend mass every Sunday in the summer at a gorgeous church within walking distance from our home. Again, the reverend was a former Catholic priest, and he was also called by his first name. I'll never forget when I broke my fingers on the tennis court and was in a cast, kneeling at the altar waiting for the host. When Denis got to me, he closed his eyes, touched my cast, and must

29

"GOOD WORKS ARE LINKS THAT FORM A CHAIN OF LOVE."

have said a prayer just for me. I was deeply moved by this. I reached out to him, too, that last summer I spent there. We talked about some of the books I was reading, like *The Power of Now* by Eckhart Tolle and *The Book of Joy* by Desmond Tutu and the Dalai Lama. Just like Jeff, he was amazing to talk to about marriage and home ownership and, quite frankly, life in general. They were both so real, you felt truly loved by them. Their kindheartedness, down-to-earth natures, and ability to empathize with their parishioners demonstrated their fundamental understanding of our daily struggles. The very last sermon I was privileged to attend was downright spooky because it was as if he was speaking directly to me. That sermon was titled "Liminal Space", which Denis described as a path we know we have to take, but because it's something new and scary and hard, we don't like the journey and the work it takes to actually get there. He went on to describe how Peter the fisherman knew what a rocky boat was because he made his living as a fisherman. But then something weird happened one day, and the security of his boat was questioned.

EXPLORE

Awake

Ben Hur

Buddha

Field of Dreams

Finding Joe

Ghost

Harold and Maude

Heal

Kramer vs. Kramer

Living with Yourself

Sister Act

Tashi and the Monk

The Color Purple

The Reality of Truth

It was Jesus appearing to him, asking Peter to step out of the boat. As long as Peter kept his eyes on Jesus, he was fine, but as soon as his focus strayed from God, he faltered and yelled out for God to save him. The sermon proceeded to describe how a hand reached out to save Peter. Then, Denis, as a magnificent reverend does, related the story to our everyday experiences. He said that when a marriage ends, it's the liminal space in a time of transition that happens to each of us. We can approach it in different ways but as soon as we take our eyes off the Lord, depression can sink in and the craziness of the action can take hold. He reminded us all to keep our eyes on the Lord and ended by encouraging us to follow Jesus, because he is holding his hand out to us always, saying *Come, come, you don't have to give into fear.* When we slip and fall his hand is out there for us. Our challenge is to keep our eyes on him. At this point, my sister-in-law, who was there with my brother and his kids and sitting one row ahead, turned around and locked eyes with me. She knew exactly how much Denis was speaking to me.

I will instruct you and teach you the way you should go; I will counsel you with my eye upon you.

Psalms 32:8

You'll hear me say a lot about how I met different people these last few years and how I went down many new avenues. While I was hiking in Santa

EXPLORE

Agape Spiritual
Center Podcast

Spirituality and
Metaphysics for
Empowerment
with Michele Meiche

Uplifted Being Show

Barbara, California, with a new friend, we got into a deep discussion about religion. After we made it to the bottom, she said, "I know exactly where I'm going to take you now!" She drove us into the middle of the gorgeous, hilly town of Montecito to a lovely little wooden temple belonging to the Vedanta Society. Inside, we took our shoes off and sat quietly for a while before going into the gift shop. While I was purchasing some CDs of Swami Tyagananda, I struck up a conversation with the volunteer. (I'm so becoming my mother, I talk to everyone now!) When she learned I lived in Boston, she told me that one of their other locations was at Boston University. Here's where I have to say that I truly believe there are no mistakes in life. I honestly know deep down in my heart that my guardian angels guided us on that detour that day. When I returned to Boston, I would alternate on Sundays between attending the Vedanta Society and listening to a kind, smiling bald man in an orange tunic, to St. Paul's

EXPLORE

Daily Word
dailyword.com

Vedanta
vedanta.org

in Chestnut Hill, Massachusetts. I felt completely comfortable in both. What I love about Vedanta is their embrace of all religions. We would begin by saying this prayer:

May there be peace on earth and in the sky.
May there be peace in the water and in all
*   directions.*
May there be peace in the plants, in the trees,
*   and in animals.*
May there be peace in the hearts of all beings.
May there be peace in everyone and in everything.

May we come together for a common purpose.
May our minds be united in the quest for
*   higher wisdom.*
Common be our prayer, common our goal.
Common our purpose, common our ideal.
Unified be our hearts, united our intentions.
Perfect be the harmony and unity amongst us.
Peace. Peace. Peace.

May the Divine Being who is:
The Father in Heaven of the Christians,

Holy One of the Jewish faith,
Allah of the Muslims,
Buddha of the Buddhists,
Dao of the Taoists,
Ahura Mazda of the Zoroastrians,
The Great Spirit of the Native Americans,
and Brahman of the Hindus,

Lead us:
from the unreal to the Real,
from darkness to Light,
from death to Immortality.

May we be granted:
strength, freedom and clear understanding.

May we learn to see God:
in our own hearts and in everyone around us.

May God bless us all:
and fill our hearts with gratitude, grace and
  love.

Peace. Peace. Peace be unto all.

One of my favorite things I learned from Swami Tyagananda was from his CD *Four Simple Exercises*:

1. Forget the good we have done for others.
2. Forget the bad that people have done to you.
3. Everything passes away—there is always impermanence.
4. Remember God alone exists—only he is constant.

I love these four deceptively simple tenets because they remind us to be charitable but not to boast about it, which is so rarely practiced in today's world. They also remind us to forgive and that things are constantly shifting, just like in the natural world.

The American Indians also have a wonderful approach to worship rooted in spiritual principles found in the natural world. They honor all living things that support their existence, especially nature and how it provides for their people. Here is an Apache prayer that I find particularly gorgeous:

May the sun bring you new energy by day.
May the moon softly restore you by night.
May the rain wash away your worries.
May the breeze blow new strength into your
    being.
May you walk gently through the world and
    know its beauty all the days of your life.

What I find so fascinating and comforting are the common threads that run between different religions and belief systems. The idea of impermanence is fundamental in each of the prayers above, from Vedanta to Catholicism to Native American spirituality. So is forgiveness and acceptance. The ultimate ideal is to seek and to adhere, as best we can, to something, even if that something is change. It doesn't matter how you package it, but it's in the seeking that we find truth and change and growth.

At one point, I even attended the Agape Congregation in Hollywood. It was during Black History Month, and the music was incredible. I struggled, however, because it was in a movie theater, and as I mentioned before I really love the feel of a traditional church with wood, stained glass windows, and the smell of incense and candles. But the biggest problem I had with my Agape experience was that an old man was sitting in front of me, and he was really into the music, I mean *really into it*, and every time he felt the spirit and stood up to dance, I got distracted. I couldn't concentrate on anything! Even though that experience nearly turned me off of Agape for good, I just this week listened to Oprah's Super Soul Conversations podcast with Michael Bernard Beckwith, the founder of Agape International Spiritual Center, and it was so incredible that I've decided to keep an open mind and give Agape one more shot.

Since I moved here to Santa Monica, I must admit I've been struggling to find the right house of worship. When my brother Johnnie was dying in his bed in the intensive care unit, his neighbor came by to visit. I didn't know at the time that she was a minister. She placed her hands on his head and said the most beautiful, touching prayers. Her energy was palpable. It was as if she was touching my head, too. Before she left, I had an intuition to exchange numbers with her, and I know my guardian angels were tapping me on the shoulder telling me to do this. I now visit her "church" in Pasadena whenever she's preaching, even if it takes me an hour to get there from Santa Monica. I put church in quotes because this one is in a movie theater, too... Oh, Hollywood. Gotta love it!

If my kids could see the places I'm going these days, they would probably be shocked since they only knew me as the mother who dragged them down the aisle of a Catholic church every Sunday for years. It's so ironic, having given away dozens of copies of Dr. Seuss's *Oh, the Places You'll Go!* at nearly every graduation and major life event for acquaintances throughout the years, that I'm the one who needs a copy today. I'm remembering now a Sunday where Kevin refused to get out of his pajamas to go to mass. I sent my husband ahead with the two older ones because I knew Kevin and I were going to butt heads. Watching us was like watch-

EXPLORE | FAITH

Visit a local church or place of worship. If the service doesn't speak to your soul, don't give up, try others. I find being in a house of worship a humbling experience and we can all use a little humility in our lives. There is nothing like a great sermon to keep you thinking throughout your week.

INSPIRATION | DR. SEUSS

"TODAY YOU ARE YOU! THAT IS TRUER THAN TRUE! THERE IS NO ONE ALIVE WHO IS YOU-ER THAN YOU!"

ing a National Geographic episode on mountain goats—a long staredown before finally digging in and taking charge. I remember thinking, "If I let him win this battle, then next Sunday the other boys will rightfully argue that they shouldn't have to go either." As a mother, I felt it was my duty to give them a religion and a faith that they could fall back on someday if and when they ever needed it. I now wish I had let Kevin win that battle. I wish I had sat on the couch, put a blanket over us, and just cuddled as I read one of his favorite books to him. He always loved non-fiction. We could have read the one about snakes and talked about how God created all creatures. Alas, I didn't, and it may be one of my few regrets in life. I've been working so hard these last few years to "have no regrets of the past, no fear of the future, and only live in the moment." However, I wish I could get that one Sunday back. It could have been a teaching moment instead of a power struggle.

All religions follow the same basic rule, which is love your creator, whatever that might look like and whatever you wish to call it, and love your neighbor. My kids don't seem to want to attend any organized religion and I understand why they might feel that way. Sometimes throughout history, we have seen power take over and muddy the waters of faith. My hope for them is that they continue to seek, regardless if they stay connected to any organized religion, because I truly believe there are gifts and profound lessons to be learned in the seeking. I'm somehow able to accept that man is imperfect and can screw it up for the rest of us. But I continue to have faith. It has gotten me through these last tough years of not knowing where I was going to live, if my children would accept my decisions, and what my future was going to hold for me, but because I have faith, it's turning out exactly as God intended. Like the sermon that Denis gave about Peter and the boat, I'm going to keep my eyes on God, even as my feet may take me in any number of different directions.

The rest of this book is about the many different things I've tried in these past few years to enhance my understanding of my spiritual life and to seek a deeper truth about who I am, the world we live in, and my place and purpose in it. Some things have worked, others have fallen flat on their faces, but one thing has remained constant, which is that I've stayed in motion. I guess you could say I'm resilient. Just like my father calling to me from across the street when I skinned my knee, I keep picking myself up and forging ahead.

PLAYLIST | PEACE

The Swan
Camille Saint-Saëns

Bridge Over Troubled Waters
Simon & Garfunkel

My Sweet Lord
George Harrison

Angel
Sarah McLachlan

Stairway to Heaven
Led Zeppelin

The Prayer
Celine Dion & Andrea Bocelli

You'll Never Walk Alone
Elvis Presley

Anchor Me
The Tenors

Amazing Grace
Judy Collins

Imagine
John Lennon

His Eye Is on the Sparrow
Whitney Houston

Somebody Bigger Than You and I
Clara Ward

Praying
Kesha

Sunday Will Never Be the Same
Spanky & Our Gang

Down to Earth
Stevie Wonder

Give Me Love
George Harrison

You're Not There
Lukas Graham

Peace Train
Cat Stevens

Gloomy Sunday
Billie Holiday

Peace
O.A.R.

Across the Universe
John Lennon

"PRAYER IS WHEN YOU TALK TO GOD; MEDITATION IS WHEN YOU LISTEN TO GOD."

MEDITATION

I started out meditating sitting cross-legged for thirty minutes at a time, and I failed miserably. I'm so competitive that I couldn't help but want to jump straight to the finish line, thinking I could simply sit down and close my eyes and be at the level of a Zen master in one week's time.

To begin with, I could not stop my thoughts for even ten seconds, let alone ten minutes, and I was so freaking uncomfortable that most of the time I was thinking about my numb left foot! The yogi term for sitting cross-legged is Padmasana, or Lotus Pose, but I call it uncomfortable. Because I started off with such high expectations of myself, in these past three years of practicing meditation, I have actually gone in reverse. Instead of sitting on the floor, I found I was more comfortable in a chair, and I went from thirty minutes down to ten. Only in the last few months have I gotten more comfortable in Lotus Pose thanks to an awesome seat that I bought online. It has a floor and back cushion, and when I'm in a good flow, practicing regularly, I can now last around twenty minutes. Is it all without thoughts entering my mind? Hell no. But I'm steadily improving, and I'm proud of that.

The first meditation course I took was with Emily Fletcher through Mindvalley's online program. Leave it to me to learn meditation from a former Rockette! She was tall, red-haired, and beautiful. It was good for me to begin meditation with someone that looked like someone I would be friends with and

EXPLORE

I Am That: Talks with Sri Nisargadatta Maharaj
Nisargadatta Maharaj

Stress Less, Accomplish More
Emily Fletcher

The Inner Game of Tennis
Timothy Gallway

Undaunted
Catherine Caine

Unplug
Suze Yalof Schwartz

Wherever You Go, There You Are
Jon Kabat-Zinn

not some bald guy in an orange robe. It demystified the process and gave it a familiar, warm face. The one thing that she often said that I loved was, "You meditate to be good at life, not to be good at meditation." Over these past three years, I have seen myself experience some things that I know I would have responded to differently before I started meditating.

I also took an online course through the Chopra Center. It was fantastic to listen to the rapport between Deepak Chopra and Oprah Winfrey. Three years later, I was able to check off an item on my bucket list which was to attend a course in California and meet Deepak. He was difficult for me to follow, quite frankly, but the people I met and the experience with my dear new California girlfriend was wonderful. Between morning and evening group meditations, yoga classes,

EXPLORE | JOURNALING

Journal exercise (based on Sanda Jasper's Reality Model): My feelings + My thoughts + My Beliefs lead to: My Choices & My Actions which create = My Reality.

Write on the following in your journal for 20 minutes. See what comes up. Ask yourself: "Is my reality being created from fear or love?"

INSPIRATION | UNKNOWN

"SOMEDAY YOU'LL LOOK BACK ON ALL OF THIS AND SMILE BECAUSE YOU DIDN'T STOP. YOU DIDN'T QUIT. EVEN WHEN THAT'S ALL YOU WANTED TO DO."

eating healthy meals, and learning new concepts, I absorbed the teachings in person more than I did in the online courses. There is something to be said about group meditations. There must be something about the collective energy in the room, because I found I was able to go deeper than when I'm alone. I found it touching to observe the few couples who attended. I actually teared up the night we did yoga outside while the sun was setting and I noticed I was surrounded in the front, back, and on both sides of me by couples that spread their blankets out to do the yoga together at sunset. It touched my heart. One day, as I was walking towards the conference room, I was in step with a man. I complimented him on being one of the few guys attending. He admitted that he was there under duress because his wife wanted him to attend with her. We laughed, but I told him sincerely that he was a good husband for doing that. Then I said, "We all know the saying, 'happy wife, happy life', and chances are huge that you'll get laid tonight." He busted out laughing even more—I don't think he was expecting that out of an attendee at the Chopra Center!

EXPLORE

The Goop Podcast

Oprah's Super Soul Conversations

Rock Your Bliss

EXPLORE

10% Happier

Headspace

Insight Timer

Calm

Breethe

If I've learned anything these past few years, it's not to lose my sense of humor with this stuff.

I was fortunate enough to travel to India and Thailand as well, where I deepened my practice with private meditation teachers. In fact, at a hotel in Mumbai where I was staying, they offered meditation each morning at six a.m. Because I'm an early riser, I welcomed the offer. As it turned out, no one else showed up, so each morning I would meet with this lovely young man who taught me a few different ways to meditate. As I'm writing this, I can still see his kind, patient face. I learned early on that there are different ways to meditate. He walked me through counting while inhaling and exhaling. He also taught me alternate nostril breathing, the process of closing one nostril at a time and inhaling and exhaling alternately. It's designed to help relieve tension and anxiety, as all forms of meditation are, but this is also great for concentration specifically, and it supposedly helps to relieve headaches. I only practice it in my apartment, because if I were to do so in public people would think I was picking my nose!

In Thailand, the yoga instructor at the hotel was also available for private meditation. He came to my room each evening and, I have to admit, I was strangely attracted to him. Some of these beautiful hotels have the most romantic bathrooms, and as he was leaving one night I was so tempted to invite him to take a bath with me. Totally inappropriate, I know, but I thought about it! After meditating with him on my balcony I was so relaxed and feeling so fantastic—but I was a good girl and refrained myself.

Another meditation teacher in Thailand, Franz, was a real character. He came to my room with props. He shared with me that he, too, struggled in the beginning, so he could totally relate to me. He pulled out a stuffed cat and mouse and said, "The cat is you, and the mouse is your thoughts. While you are meditating, that mouse can start to scurry around. The trick is for you, as the cat, to reach

EXPLORE | BREATHING

Thich Nhat Hanh gave the best advice yet that I've found on breathing. He suggests while breathing in to simply think "I'm breathing in" and while exhaling to simply think "I'm breathing out."

53

out to the mouse and pull him in." My thoughts can move from mundane things like what am I going to eat next to what groceries I need to buy, or I can be deep in thought about my relationships with my three sons, the wonderful holidays we've shared or a specific memory of feeling proud of their accomplishments, and suddenly that memory shifts to wondering if they blame me for ruining their beliefs of marriage. It happens in an instant. What meditation does is help slow me down and identify when it's actually happening. I still use the visualization technique that Franz taught me because it continues to work. I shared with him that although I didn't have a problem sitting still, I preferred to be outdoors in nature. He thought that was a great insight.

The next day, instead of meeting in my hotel room, we met for a bike ride and a hike. It was perhaps the most memorable holiday experience of my life so far. The bike ride there was gorgeous, passing temples along the way, and we had some

EXPLORE

Avatar

Free Solo

Inner Worlds, Outer Worlds

Karate Kid

Life of Pi

Little Buddha

The Dawn Wall

The Dhamma Brothers

Waking Life

EXPLORE

#zivameditation
#buddhism_meditation
#dharmav1bes
#meditationspace

of the deepest conversations I've ever had with a man. He would look up at a tree and say things like, "See how that branch seems to be missing a leaf? That allows the sunlight to come through and warm the earth below the tree. It also allows another leaf to grow." Things like this he would point out along our walk. I shared with him that I was getting divorced. He, too, had gone through that experience. He told me he had a daughter who was initially very angry with him but eventually came around, and they were ultimately able to rekindle their father-daughter friendship. That brought me solace and relieved a lot of anxiety for me.

Then, he gave me a lesson that I'm forever grateful for, a visualization that I've used many times in the last three years. He had been walking not with a stick but with one ski pole. Sure, I may have been through a mid-life crisis, but this man had been a firefighter in the Netherlands and decided to leave his wife to move to Chaing Mai, Thailand, shave his head, and become a priest. My moving from Massachusetts to California was nothing compared to that! He told me to stay standing where I was, walked a few yards ahead of me, and pushed the ski pole into the ground along the hiking path. Then he walked back to me.

"You see that pole in the distance?" he asked.

"Yes," I said.

"That's where you want to get to eventually," he said. "Now, together, let's take one step."

He asked me to look around to see what I saw. We paused. He even pointed out a flower that he had never noticed before even though he had done this particular hike many times. He said, "Look behind you." I turned and did what he asked. Then he said, "You were back there, but you aren't anymore, are you?" He wanted me to stop and celebrate that one step forward. I felt like a little grasshopper listening and learning as a child does. He then made me look to where the pole was waiting patiently. "But," he said, "you are closer to your goal." He did this for a few more steps and suddenly my situation crystallized. At that time in my life, I wasn't sure where I was going to live, what my sons were going to do because we hadn't told them yet, and what the timing of all this was going to be. It was a very stressful time in my life and walking in nature

INSPIRATION | DR. MARTIN LUTHER KING, JR.

"IF YOU CAN'T FLY THEN RUN, IF YOU CAN'T RUN THEN WALK, IF YOU CAN'T WALK THEN CRAWL, BUT WHAT-EVER YOU DO YOU HAVE TO KEEP MOVING FORWARD."

EXPLORE

Chopra Center
chopra.com

DailyOM
dailyom.com

Gaia
gaia.com

MindValley
mindvalley.com

Roger Gabriel
rogergabriel.com

with this kindhearted, gentle giant brought me solace.

As we were reaching the summit it began to pour rain. We laughed, and he asked me if I wanted to run back. I love the rain, and I love a windy day. "Hell no!" I said. We laughed as we continued getting drenched. Later, he turned me onto the heart mantra *Om Mani Padme Hum*. You have to sound it out. Its lesson is about learning how to give. As the sound vibrates out of your body, energy vibrates out. You are literally creating and giving the world energy. Even when you are listening to it online, you can create the same experience as you would with a group of monks in a monastery, especially if you do it with noise-canceling headphones.

As I have been exploring these different avenues, I continue meeting people with very different interests and histories than I associated with in my past. My Qigong master, Beverly, once said to me, "Watch: as you become more authentic, you will vibrationally meet people who are more in tune with you." She was correct (as always!). The more I embrace and put the heart mantra to practice, the more I see exactly what Beverly was saying. For instance, I recently signed up for some Meetups, which is an app that connects people with similar interests. I attended a spiritual book club, and I'm so glad I did. We met at a cool coffee shop in West Hollywood and discussed the book *Undaunted* by Christine Caine. I enjoyed the discussions and the people were lovely.

I'm listening now to *Unplug* by Suze Yalof Schwartz. She makes meditation accessible, and she illustrates what I've experienced in the last three years, which is that there are many ways to meditate. I'm constantly trying new approaches. At times I'm inside, other times I'm on the grass or sand; I count when I need to, I use visualization when the day calls for it (my favorite is the sun rising over the mountains in Bhutan when I was there hiking), I

EXPLORE | AROMATHERAPY

Muji is one of my favorite stores where I bought a fantastic room vaporizer. I also buy my essential oils anywhere in Santa Monica or online. I love frankincense, eucalyptus, and ylang ylang. The aromas, like incense, create a sensory experience which can help to deepen the meditation experience.

use alternate nostril breathing (only in private!), guided online meditations, and subject-based meditations found on various apps. Like I said, I started out trying desperately to do thirty minutes and went backwards to ten minutes. I've since settled somewhere around twenty minutes. The important thing is to try it. I liked learning from *Unplug* that even Pete Carroll, coach of the Seattle Seahawks (who used to coach the Patriots and whom I've had a crush on ever since), wanted his whole team to practice meditation because it helps with focus. I wish I had been turned on to it sooner. It could have helped me when I was playing team tennis, and God knows I was an emotional mess then. Friends kept giving me the book *The Inner Game of Tennis* by Timothy Gallwey because I was such a basket case! I must have three copies of it somewhere in my storage unit along with some fancy clothes and high-heeled shoes that I never wear anymore. His book describes how you have to be in the now and focus, which is exactly what meditation does.

Another point Schwartz makes is how meditation is like a muscle: the more you work it, the stronger it becomes. Remember the saying, "No pain no gain"?

One morning I had a particularly hard time meditating. I try not to get discouraged because I know there are people who have been practicing for over thirty years who still struggle, and I just started, but later that morning, while I was volunteering at my local food pantry in Venice Beach, I noticed something that made me realize that my daily practice was finally clicking. I usually work on a Monday morning and truly love the other volunteers that I work with, but since I had been in San Francisco to watch our beloved Patriots win another Super Bowl, I said I'd work on Friday that week instead. When I arrived, I met an older Japanese woman who was both extraordinarily nice and a complete and total control freak. You know the type? She proceeded

EXPLORE | VISUALIZATION

Here is a trick I learned way too late in life but I'm so glad I learned it. Ever notice when you are with someone who is negative they suck the energy out of you? I totally have experienced this. I've walked away feeling physically depleted. What I do now is I visualize a sheaf around me. You can picture it white or lavender. The concept is that their negative energy can't enter your field. Don't allow it baby! Don't you freaking allow their negative energy to enter you.

EXPLORE

Deva Premal: Om-
Mani-Padme-Hum
youtube.com/watch?
v=l4oy17lwVnM

Gaia: "This is Your
Brain on Meditation"
with Joe Dispenza
gaia.com/video/
your-brain-meditation-
joe-dispenza

Oprah Winfrey:
Thich Nhat Hanh
youtube.com/watch?
v=NJ9UtuWfs3U

to tell me exactly how to open a plastic bag and exactly how she wanted me to place the lettuce into the bags. At one point, I was chatting with a young man who was learning to cook at the shelter so he could eventually find work in the food industry. We were sharing favorite recipes and laughing a lot, and then, just like schoolchildren, we were scolded. We were told we were there to work and not to have fun. In years past, the old Megan would have said something to her. Instead, I just smiled and did what I was told to do. Later, she explained to me that she previously worked in a job that required precise organizational skills. I was kind and said that she must have been very good at what she did and how lucky we were at the food pantry to benefit from her skills. When my shift was over, she literally spread her arms wide, gave me a big smile, and hugged me. I was shocked. She said it was a delight working with me and that she hoped I would come back again on a Friday. When I shared this story on Monday with my usual volunteer peeps, they were like, "Oh no, we should have told you no one wants to work on Fridays because of her. How did you survive that?" I'm telling you, just when I think I'm not getting the meditation thing, something like this happens and I realize that it is helping me become a better, calmer person. And for that I'm truly grateful.

PLAYLIST | ZEN

I Am a Rock
Simon & Garfunkel

Smile
Rod Stewart

Mean Old World
Sam Cooke

The Rose
Bette Midler

I'm So Lonesome
I Could Cry
Willie Nelson

Wild Flower
New Birth

Rainbow
Kasey Musgraves

Butterflies
Kasey Musgraves

You Say
Lauren Daigle

Three Little Birds
Bob Marley

Don't Worry,
Be Happy
Bobby McFerrin

Anticipation
Carly Simon

What a Difference
a Day Makes
Dinah Washington

Stand by Me
Sam Cooke

I'll Be There
Jackson 5

Hero
Mariah Carey

Thank You
Sly & the Family
Stone

Call on Me
Big Brother and the
Holding Company

Let It Be
The Beatles

A Change Is
Gonna Come
Sam Cooke

03.

"YOU'VE ALWAYS HAD THE POWER, MY DEAR, YOU JUST NEEDED TO LEARN IT FOR YOURSELF."

ENERGY

Tai Chi

In the past few years I've been exposed to many types of energy practices that I had never even heard of before. One morning in 2017, while walking around the Public Garden in Boston listening to the audio version of *The Book of Joy* by the Dalai Lama and Desmond Tutu, I stumbled upon a circle of Asian women doing some form of exercise.

I was fascinated by their camaraderie and I stopped to watch. I felt funny joining their circle, so I stood

EXPLORE

The Chakra Handbook
Shalila Sharamon
and Bodo J. Baginski

Chakras for Beginners
David Pond

Seat of the Soul
Gary Zukav
(Audiobook)

The God Effect:
Quantum
Entanglement
Brian Clegg

The Laws of Attraction:
The Basics of the
Teachings of Abraham
Esther and Jerry Hicks
(Audiobook)

a little away from them doing whatever the leader did. She kept looking over at me and smiling. When they finished, I went to thank her and felt this need to touch her. As I rubbed her shoulder and thanked her, I thought she was trying to tell me to join them the next day. She called her friend over to interpret. I was told they were doing Tai Chi which, according to Wikipedia, "is an internal Chinese martial art practiced for both its defense training and its health benefits. The term 'taiji' refers to a philosophy of the forces of yin and yang, related to the moves."

So I joined the "Asian Grandmothers", as I affectionately called them, the next day and every day after for Tai Chi by the swan boats. The first day I felt they were a bit quiet and I felt badly, but the more I showed up, the more comfortable they became with me and vice versa. They assembled every morning at

7:00 a.m., and there was a gentleman who would join them punctually at 7:30 a.m. He arrived on his bike wearing pressed khaki pants, a tailored white shirt, and a wonderful old straw hat. He would take off his shoes, pull a handkerchief out of his bike basket, dip it into the pond, and methodically clean the stone bench in front of where he exercised. He did more sophisticated moves than we did and was mesmerizing to watch.

I adored these women. They greeted me each morning with a big smile and an enthusiastic "Hi–good morning!" They didn't speak any other English. I loved how they talked and laughed with each other throughout the workout, and there I was between them, happily listening and sharing their energy as we followed our fantastic guide who had the most beautiful smile.

One day, at the end, one of the women was going around offering candy. I said no, but I quickly realized the mistake I had made. When families and communities gather, they often share a meal (think of dinner with families or at church when sharing the host). It brings people together. Well I'll be damned if the leader didn't notice my face when

I realized I had made a mistake by declining. She nodded, grabbed two from the woman, and handed them to me with a smile.

Oh, how loved I felt in her presence. I was just amazed at the practice. We touched, tapped, and stroked every inch of our bodies. There are some movements that reminded me of daily hygiene and it all made so much sense, a cleansing on so many levels. At one point, I thought we looked like we were literally brushing our hair, and washing our faces, ears, and teeth with our tongues. The leader's granddaughter was there another day and she and I really connected. While I did the different motions she would describe what she saw. All of a sudden, she squealed with laughter and said, "Now you are holding a balloon!" A few moments later, a beaming smile still on her face, "You are pushing the clouds away." Those images have stuck with me ever since, and I love how perfect it felt coming from a child. I would always leave there with such a surge of energy!

I feel like my stumbling onto those fantastic Asian Grandmothers was a big step for me. As I was working my way towards enlightenment and finding the new me without country clubs or working out in gyms, I made a step towards my goal of being by myself (and enjoying it). I had the courage to stop when I first saw those women, and I am so grateful for that. I felt their amazing energy, and even though our gatherings have ended, the sense of loving energy has stayed with me. And I swear it gave me the energy I needed to start writing again. I had been stewing over a book idea for a long time, but after practicing Tai Chi with those women I was finally able to sit down and begin the book you're reading now.

Qigong

My guardian angels were constantly feeding me new information and introducing new people into my life for me to learn from. For so long, I felt I was on auto-pilot with a hole inside of me. Through these new experiences, I was searching for a way to fill that hole.

A new friend I made on my incredible trip halfway around the world turned me onto her Qigong master (pronounced "chē-gong"). When I first called her, I

INSPIRATION | UNKNOWN

"WHEN YOU REPLACE 'WHY IS THIS HAPPENING TO ME?' WITH 'WHAT IS THIS TRYING TO TEACH ME?' EVERYTHING SHIFTS."

was amazed at all she knew of my situation without my telling her much and how calm I felt after we talked. Then, my first trip to see her was absolutely wild. She basically said I was a complete mess. She asked for permission to "work on me" then proceeded to make these switching motions as she tried to clear the gunk stuck inside of me that kept my energy from flowing.

I can still see Beverly looking deeply into my eyes that first time and saying, "I wish you could see what I see." She said that I had the most gorgeous soul she had ever seen. She described it as a beautiful woman with long flowing hair in a white dress walking barefoot in a field of wildflowers. "But there is a thing called momentum," she said, "and if you have a sixteen-ton train sitting on a track for a long time it takes a great deal of energy to get the train to even start moving, but once it's moving it takes less energy to get it to go faster. The hard part is the very first step of forward motion."

It was she who introduced me to the idea of my soul. For the first time, I wanted to make that soulful woman inside me happy and do all that I could so that she could experience a joy in the next life after

EXPLORE

#lawsofattraction

#lawofattraction_peace

#affirmations_
lawsofattraction

#manifest.the.law.
of.attraction

#mimikuodeemer

#crystalreikihealer

#crystalxcactus

#thethoughtspower

my body left this earth. I was ready to take that first step. At the end of the first session (I try to visit her once a year now to clear my chakras as best she can), she stood over me and said a prayer. I began to sob. I couldn't stop. I kept repeating, "I hate to cry, I hate to cry, I hate to cry." I grew up in a household where crying was not allowed, so I was never the type of girlfriend that would cry after a breakup. Instead, I would crank my music really loud in my bedroom as I laced up my sneakers. Since this was before Walkmen and cell phones, I would keep that last song in my mind as I ran for miles. Once, I remember finding myself four towns away from my home, thinking, "Oh crap, now I have to get back home." (This was long before Uber, too!) While I was crying in Beverly's lovely office, she kept saying to me, "You need to cry. Get that crap out of you." Apparently, I have been keeping lifetimes of tears and heartache inside of me which was causing lots of blockage.

Female Qigong masters are very rare, so leave it to me to find one who not only is a woman, but who is a regular kind of gal who curses and scolds me like a mother or close friend. She's the one who guided me through big decisions like how to leave possessions behind that had bad energy attached to them and how to become my authentic self. She reminded me that I am a good decision maker and to trust my gut. When I found my dream apartment and decided to move to Santa Monica, she applauded me.

I once told her that I wished I wasn't such a tough ass. She almost yelled at me, saying, "It's your strength that has kept you alive. I wouldn't have taken you on if I didn't like that about you!"

Tarot Cards

I've been getting my tarot cards read for years. Like anything, some readers are better than others. I guess you could argue that the weaker readings happen when I'm not as mindful as I could be while holding the deck of cards and splitting them. It's all about the energy you put forth.

I know many people are skeptical, but I was amazed at my last two readings because these women saw things that in fact did happen. One woman I met in Del Mar, California, was so spooky good I made all of my siblings visit her. My brother Johnnie was always a scaredy-cat and refused to go to her, so he sent his wife instead! She told my sister-in-law that Johnnie's heart and liver weren't good. She told her to watch him during his sleep. Two years later, in the middle of the night, Johnnie died of a brain hemorrhage.

When I saw her, she looked in my eyes, actually she kept asking me to move my hair away from my forehead as she focused on the spot between my eyebrows (my third eye), and the first thing she said to me was, "Dear, I'm sorry to tell you this, but you have aged five years in one year. At that moment, I imagined a cartoon bubble above her head translating what she said to, "Sorry, my dear, but you look like shit!" Then she said that I had built too many walls inside of me. She kept telling me I needed to break down those walls. I'm sure she was right. I keep a lot inside and I've always thought that was a good thing. I hate chicks who whine. I usually try to just keep it inside and move on, but now I'm learning for the first time that that shit builds up and is not good to keep inside of you. I wish I had been turned on to this stuff when I was younger.

My girlfriends know whenever we go on our girls' weekend trips that if we pass a tarot card reader I'm going to force them to pull over. They always tell you not to share the reading with anyone, but we never listen to that. We talk about it for hours afterwards as we raid the minibar in our hotel rooms. Every time we go, something turns out to be true. Tarot readings give us a glimpse of a potential future and stoke our imaginations. And they cautiously encourage and guide us forward.

Feng Shui

I moved into our Boston apartment and although I had chosen everything, I still felt my husband's energy in it, so I googled local Feng Shui specialists. Of all of the ones to choose from, I was amazed by the woman who entered the apartment. Both of us instantly felt the energy charge between us.

Again, I felt so strongly that my guardian angels guided me directly to her. She was a mother of kids the same ages as mine. As we talked, she shared how she became a specialist in the field. One day she was at the recycling center and she happened upon a book about Feng Shui. We laughed as she said she discovered her fate at the local dump! I mean you can't make this stuff up! She instantly became obsessed with learning as much as she could.

Did it work for me? I don't know. I think the pivotal moment came when I was asking my angels for a sign as to whether I should stay in the apartment or move. I went to bed praying for that sign. The next morning, I woke up to a bug the size of my fist on my kitchen window sill. I wrapped it in a paper towel and carried it down to the doorman.

He said, "Mrs. O'Block, this is a flying cockroach. I have never seen one in this building before."

I immediately called my friend and said, "Do you think this is a sign?"

"Of course it is a sign!" she said. "What would we do back in Hoboken when we saw a cockroach?"

"Run?" I said.

"Yes!" she screamed. "*Run!*"

INSPIRATION | JOSEPH CAMPBELL

"WE MUST BE WILLING TO GET RID OF THE LIFE WE'VE PLANNED SO AS TO HAVE THE LIFE THAT IS WAITING FOR US."

Chakras

I was first introduced to chakras by a Scottish flight attendant when I had the amazing experience of traveling halfway around the world. Whenever Louise had a moment, she and I would talk, and she taught me something new every time. She walked me through the chakras and the words to say while meditating and visualizing each chakra.

Every day she would bring her cards of inspiration and ask me to pick one. One day I chose "Metamorphosis: Within myself is always awareness and opportunity to make choices that promote personal transformation", which eventually gave me the idea for the title of this book.

The chakras vibrate at different speeds depending on their color: Red, Orange, Yellow, Green, Blue, Indigo, and Lavender. Interestingly, men's chakras rotate in the opposite direction from women's. That's no surprise to me. I've always believed in that saying, "Men are from Mars, women are from Venus."

Like I've said, I am new to it and find it complex because there is so much to it, so Beverly suggested

I purchase *The Chakra Handbook* by Shalila Shar-amon and Bodo J. Baginski. Just like in college, my copy is full of underlined passages and notes in the margins. I was told recently by Sanda, my psychol-ogist and spiritual guru, that my yellow chakra was off balance. At first, I was annoyed, because I've always felt I was a good decision maker, but Sanda said I make too many decisions based on my brain and not on my heart. So, I referred back to this book and found this paragraph which hit me like a ton of bricks. It said that when the yellow or Solar Plexus chakra is disharmonious, it may be because you are driven by an inner restlessness and discontent:

EXPLORE | CHAKRAS

Check your closet. If you need more colors to express your moods and areas of your chakras that need attention go to stores like Uniqlo and buy some colored t-shirts! Start to consider wearing less black as it closes energy from entering your system. White, however, is a great color to wear as it emits all the colors of the rainbow.

Practice this heart chakra exercise. If there is someone you love whom you want to send a message, you can use visualization. Focus on your heart chakra, think of the color green, picture them there at your heart center literally meditating and taking deep long breaths. Allow your loving energy from your heart to envelop them.

"You probably experienced a lack of acceptance during your childhood years and adolescence. Acceptance and material well-being are of primary importance for you, and perhaps you are quite successful in obtaining them. As a consequence, your emotions are stopped-up. But occasionally they break through this wall of control and defense like a flood, making it impossible for you to channel them correctly. You get highly upset easily, but your agitation is an expression of all the anger you have swallowed over a long period of time.

One day you will finally have to acknowledge that striving for material wealth and recognition cannot provide you with true long-term satisfaction."

Apparently, sunlight is crucial for my well-being, which is just another validation that I made the right decision to move to California! Because of my yellow chakra imbalance, I was recently out shopping with my niece and I told her I needed a yellow t-shirt, so

EXPLORE | CHAKRA CHART

CROWN
SAHASRARA

The crown (**7th chakra**) is located at the top of the head. It represents states of higher consciousness and divine connection. Imbalanced attributes would be cynicism, closed mindedness, and disconnection with spirit. Color: **Lavender**. Mantra: **OM**.

THIRD EYE
AJNA

The third eye (**6th chakra**) is located in the center of the forehead, between the eyebrows. It represents intuition, foresight, and is driven by openness and imagination. Imbalanced attributes would be lack of direction and clarity. Color: **Indigo**. Mantra: **OM**.

THROAT
VISSUDHA

The throat (**5th chakra**) is located at the center of the neck. It represents the ability to communicate clearly and effectively. Imbalanced attributes would be shyness, being withdrawn, arrogance, and increased anxiety. Color: **Blue**. Mantra: **HAM**.

HEART
ANAHATA

The heart (**4th chakra**) is located in the center of the chest. It represents love, self-love, and governs our relationships. Imbalanced attributes would be depression, difficulty in relationships, and lack of self-discipline. Color: **Green**. Mantra: **YAM**.

SOLAR PLEXUS
MANIPURA

The solar plexus (**3rd chakra**) is located below the chest. It represents self-esteem, pleasure, will-power, and personal responsibility. Imbalanced attributes would be low self-esteem, control issues, and manipulative tendencies. Color: **Yellow**. Mantra: **RAM**.

SACRAL
SWADHISTHANA

The sacral (**2nd chakra**) is located below the navel. It represents creative and sexual energies. Imbalanced attributes would be lack of or repressed creativity, sexual dysfunction, witheld intimacy, and emotional isolation. Color: **Orange**. Mantra: **VAM**.

ROOT
MULADHARA

The root (**1st chakra**) is located at the base of the spine. It provides the foundation on which we build our life—representing safety, security, and stability. Imbalanced attributes would be scattered energies, anxiety, and fear. Color: **Red**. Mantra: **LAM**.

we stopped in one of my new favorite stores, Uniqlo, and bought matching yellow t-shirts for a whopping $9.90 each!

I have learned and changed so much during these past two years. I used to wear the color black most of the time. Now, since learning about chakras, I find myself deciding what color to wear based on my mood, and although I still hate to shop, if I do, now I find myself buying clothes in colors other than black. But real change takes more than wearing different clothes on different days. For real change to happen, you need to change your thoughts and attitudes, which elevate emotions like gratitude and joy. When you feel this, you switch on new waves and elevated emotions carry a different frequency. You become more energy, more mind, more matter. When I come across someone who is truly awakened because of this stuff, I always think of that classic scene in *When Harry Met Sally* when Meg Ryan fakes an orgasm in public, and the older woman beside her in the diner says, "I'll have what she's having." I mean, who wouldn't want to try this stuff if all of this bliss is promised to us?

EXPLORE

Blue Planet
Fatal Attraction
Laws of Attraction
The Wizard of Oz
When Harry Met Sally

Reiki

On another one of my soul-searching walks along the Charles River, I was trying to figure out what I really enjoyed doing and how I could really make a difference. Suddenly, I remembered how I loved holding babies. I loved the smell of them and their delicious softness.

My mother used to give me a hard time because I held my three sons so much. She was one of those mothers who had six children but rarely ever held us because she was so busy. She once tried to teach me how to "prop" a bottle. I remember saying, "Mom, this is my favorite time of the day. Why the hell would I roll a towel under his chin so that the bottle could fit into his mouth only so I can walk away from him?"

I probably think back on those days too often, but I have absolutely no regrets of the time I spent holding them close to my body.

With those warm thoughts in mind, I researched volunteer opportunities for holding premature babies at a nearby hospital. I learned that was the one area that was very hard to volunteer for because so many people want to do it. At fourteen years old, I was, for a very brief time, what we used to call a "candy striper". We were young girls who volunteered at the hospital and wore these hideous pink and white striped aprons. Unfortunately, I was assigned the old people's ward and after just one day of seeing old men's asses with their blue gowns open in the back, I walked the hell out of that hospital and never returned. I was such a badass then, I didn't even finish my shift; I just walked out!

Anyhow, I learned that if you completed your second level of Reiki certification you were more likely to be chosen by the hospital for the premature baby positions. So, of course, being the chick that

---

EXPLORE | ENERGY

Visit a crystal store. Ask questions. Buy one that best suits where you're at and what you're working on.

Take a Tai Chi class.

Have your home assessed by a Feng Shui specialist. They will make valuable suggestions to you for changing the energy in your home or workspace.

Get a tarot card reading. It's fascinating to hear what they may see for your immediate future.

EXPLORE

The Energy
Healing Podcast
with Tara Williams

The Energy
Blueprint Podcast
with Ari Whitten

sets goals and figures out what steps to take to achieve them, I went and got my second level of certification in Reiki.

I was trained by a husband and wife team, and throughout this journey I've crossed paths with many couples who work together in herbal medicine, Reiki, and acupuncture. They gave me separate Reiki treatments, and I found it fascinating that they both said my throat chakra was "murky". Apparently, they see different colors associated with different body parts and chakras, and they can also tell if it's bright or cloudy, dark or blocked.

I was experimenting with so many things, as you have read, but I have to admit I did not stick with Reiki. It's something you have to practice and truly integrate into your life. I did, however, get chosen to be a volunteer in the intensive care unit for newborns. It was such an honor, but that week I also made the huge decision to leave Boston and move to California, so I never did get to

EXPLORE

Chakra Clearing
youtube.com/
watch?v=RhZfulT4zSE

Raise Positive
Energy and Remove
Negative Energy
youtube.com/watch?v=
gRhUvHGKWHE

experience that wonderful opportunity. But again, I go back to my blueprint: perhaps it wasn't the final destination of practicing Reiki regularly, but the journey of discovering it that mattered.

Crystals

The best massage of my life was on a yoga retreat in Mexico. The masseuse's specialty was working with crystals. I started on my stomach as she covered my body with oil, especially my ass, because I said my left cheek was hurting! She then had me flip over and she covered my pelvic area with a white linen cloth.

I remember this experience because it touched all of my senses. The room didn't have windows, so you could hear the birds and feel the gentle breeze. I could smell the ylang ylang oil she expertly rubbed on my arms, legs, and feet. She placed crystals from my forehead down my throat and all over my chest to my belly button. Every so often she would pause and rearrange them.

INSPIRATION | MAHATMAS GANDHI

"KEEP YOUR THOUGHTS POSITIVE BECAUSE YOUR THOUGHTS BECOME YOUR WORDS.

KEEP YOUR WORDS POSITIVE BECAUSE YOUR WORDS BECOME YOUR BEHAVIOR.

KEEP YOUR BEHAVIOR POSITIVE BECAUSE YOUR BEHAVIOR BECOMES YOUR HABITS.

KEEP YOUR HABITS POSITIVE BECAUSE YOUR HABITS BECOME YOUR VALUES.

KEEP YOUR VALUES POSITIVE BECAUSE YOUR VALUES BECOME YOUR DESTINY."

When she was done, she placed the crystals on a table in the order in which they were on my body. She described the red crystal that she had placed on my belly button in detail. She regretted our time was up, because she felt strongly that the red crystal wanted to stay there longer. I asked what that meant and she said something about my umbilical cord. I shared with her then and only then that I had just gotten divorced, and although my sons were older, I was deeply concerned about the pain they were feeling and wanted them to know I would never abandon them. She responded almost nonchalantly and said, "Oh, well then, that all makes sense." She said because I was open and receptive to crystal energy that the crystals placed themselves exactly where the healing needed to happen.

The Reiki couple told me to buy blue agate and place it on my throat while lying down. I remember thinking it was actually a good thing that I lived alone because if I was with a man he would assume I was completely off my rocker! And I currently carry around a rose quartz, which is a stone to help heal love and attract love. I have bought many of them because I keep leaving them in my jeans and losing them in my washing machine. I love living in California for so many reasons, one of which is that there are crystal stores on nearly every corner.

PLAYLIST | CONNECT

Que Sera, Sera
Mellymaus &
Friends

I Wish I Knew
How It Would Feel
to Be Free
Nina Simone

Don't You
Worry About
a Thing
Stevie Wonder

Lean on Me
Bill Withers

I'll Be There
Jackson 5

O-o-h Child
The Five Stairsteps

I'll Stand by You
The Pretenders

Wind Beneath
My Wings
Bette Midler

You've Got
a Friend
Carol King

I'll Be There
Jess Glynne

Put Your
Records On
Corinne Bailey Rae

That's Life
Frank Sinatra

Feel This Moment
Pitbull (feat.
Christina Aguilera)

That's the Way
of the World
Earth, Wind & Fire

It Was So Easy Then
Carly Simon

Alive
Sia

Supernova
Liz Phair

"MATHEMATICS IS THE LANGUAGE IN WHICH GOD HAS WRITTEN THE UNIVERSE."

NUMEROLOGY

Numerology might be the thing that has spoken to me the most this past year. The coincidences I continue to experience with numbers are too much to deny. It's crazy. But real. The most profound experience was when it happened as my brother Johnnie was dying and in the days that followed. Everything was so synchronous that I had no choice but to take it as a sign from above.

Here are a couple of journal entries from that time:

11/9/18
1:11 a.m. *Just got a call from Ernie that Johnnie's on his way to the hospital. Gemma called him hysterical that Johnnie's heart stopped. Please, dear God, don't take my Johnnie. I love him so much.*

After I got the call at 1:11, I swear, Johnnie, you know I believe in all this freaky stuff, but I want to thank you for visiting me in my dream. I'm quite certain you died immediately and you came to me. I tried not to go back to sleep but I must have dozed off because I had this crazy vivid dream where you were dancing down a hallway of a hotel and I was running towards you, and while I hugged you I kept saying, "Johnnie, Oh Johnnie, I was looking for you, where'd you go?" And you were so happy and laughing at me. I felt you and jumped awake.

I'm on my flight from MX to LAX. Will sleep

*in a chair next to Johnnie tonight. Kitten,
Ernie, Jason, and Gemma have been by his
side all day. We're all devastated. He is
everybody's favorite. I texted my boys and
their spouses. Rob responded immediately.
Then Maggie then Jeffery which was sweet.
Kevin always surprises me. His text said,
"I'm sorry, I'm here if you want to talk." He
said the same thing when I had to put down
our family dog, Gwen. I didn't call because I
was sobbing, but I've always regretted that,
so this time I did. We had a nice conversation. I told him how much I appreciated that.
He ended our call with "I love you." Johnnie
will like hearing that.*

11/11/18
We turned off Johnnie's life support.

11/16/18
1:11 p.m. *As I was walking home from my
hair appointment listening to Carly Simon's*
Danny Boy, *I was praying my Hail Mary's
and to my "army" of angels and asking God*

*to take my Johnnie directly to Heaven. I said
to my mother, "Johnnie is on his way". I said
to God that Johnnie was such a kind, gentle
soul that if there is such a thing as reincar-
nation that I was pretty sure that Johnny
was taken from this earth early because he
was "done" and that he was a perfect being
so that he would go directly to Heaven. All
this year I have been asking my guardian
angels to send me signs and that I would
be open to listening to them. I looked at my
phone and it said 1:11. I thanked them. I
believe that was their sign telling me that
that is exactly what happened—that he is
happy in Heaven in God's beautiful home.*

Horoscope/
Astrological Chart

**Every so often I get my astrological chart read. The person I
use is Chris Flisher, but there are many other great options**

EXPLORE

How To Read the
Akashic Records
Bill Foss

Many Lives,
Many Masters
Dr. Brian Weiss

out there. After you send him your exact date of birth plus the exact time, he analyzes it and then schedules a call to go over it with you. If you don't know the exact time of your birth you can get it from the hospital where you were born. It's fascinating because it's about numbers, science, and the stars; it's mathematical.

My recent reading blew me away. Again, I don't tell these people anything beforehand. The really good ones will actually stop you if you do.

Chris was saying things about the position of Mercury and how it is affecting my life this year.

"Did you experience many changes in your life around twenty-eight years ago?" he asked me.

"Ah yeah," I said. "I moved, got married, and started having children."

He said, "And now, twenty-eight years later, would you say you are experiencing changes again?"

EXPLORE

The Daily Horoscope
Numerology Secrets
TimePassages

"Ah yeah," I repeated. "I moved, got divorced, and went through menopause."

He went on to say that was

exactly what my chart was showing. I asked him if I should have made changes sooner and he adamantly felt that that would not have worked. In fact, he reassured me that I was moving along exactly how I was intended to. It reminded me of my conversation about blueprints with Nicole from the Aura Shop in Venice and brought me great comfort.

Akashic Records

Early on in my journey a friend introduced me to a woman who specializes in Akashic Records, which are essentially the collective whole of all human events throughout the history of the world, including all thoughts, emotions, and actions to have occurred in the past or to occur in the future. It's everything that's ever been thought, said, or done, and everything that will be.

She was an incredibly intuitive woman. Every so often, when something really hit her, she would get up and pace the room. She felt very strongly that in my past lives I served in various spiritual capacities. She said I was a nun, a priest, and an herbal medicine practitioner. She said we meet people in this life who were in our lives in the past. She kept walking around saying, "Travel. I want you to travel." And she repeatedly heard my mother. In those days, early on in my journey, I was regularly praying to my mother. I kept wishing she was still alive because I wanted her advice. On days when I begged her to visit me,

EXPLORE

Astrological chart/
horoscope
chris-flisher-turning-
of-the-wheel.com

astrology-numerology.
com/numerology.html

Journey to the
Akashic Records
with Bill Foss
gaia.com/video/
exploring-akashic-
records-bill-foss

Subscribe to DailyOM
for daily horoscopes
dailyom.com/cgi-bin/
userinfo/settings.cgi

Numerology report
video.numerologist.com

I'll be damned if I didn't find a penny in my path. All of a sudden, this woman said, "*Pennies, Pennies from Heaven*, I don't know why I'm hearing that song." I had never once mentioned anything to her about my mother and my penny experience.

EXPLORE

The Numerology Chick
with Natalie Pescetti

The Astrology Podcast
with Chris Brennan

That experience was strong enough that I signed up for a weekend course on Akashic Records, but like a lot of the things I've explored, I didn't stick with it. In an exercise where we worked on each other, I didn't feel a thing. One woman there was excellent, but ultimately it was just one of many explorations and learning experiences I've had along the way.

Past Lives

One weekend not too long ago, my puppy Paco and I drove to Palm Springs just for the hell of it. I absolutely love my new life—I have no strings attached and when the spirit moves us we just get into my red jeep and drive. Paco's a perfect partner, too, because he's always up for going anywhere with me!

That night after dinner, we walked around the town, and I realized one of the reasons I love California is because they love dogs and let you bring them almost anywhere. We passed a wonderful store that sold crystals and essential oils, and they also

EXPLORE

#numerology1010

#dailyom

#awakened_soul_1111

#higherawakening

EXPLORE

A Beautiful Mind
Cloud Atlas
Good Will Hunting
Pi
The Imitation Game
The Man Who Knew Infinity
The Matrix
The Theory of Everything

offered past life tarot readings. Since I have had my regular tarot cards read many times, I decided to try one based on past lives. I'm always open to new experiences; I thrive on them. It's crazy to think of all the new things I've experienced in these past two years compared with the previous twenty years.

Much like regular tarot cards, I closed my eyes and really embraced the moment while holding the cards. She then had me choose cards and flip them over one at a time as she analyzed them. Another freaking amazing experience. She felt strongly that

EXPLORE | NUMEROLOGY

Have your Astrological Chart read. Get your exact time of birth if you don't already know it, and then have your astrological chart read: astromark.us/what-if-i-dont-know-my-birth-time/.

Have your Akashic Chart read. Research Akashic Records specialists near you: lifeintegrity.com.

Research Past Lives. Some hypnotists do this work as well.

when I drew the card with a shield and sword that it told her I was instrumental in fighting for religious freedom in a past life. Later, when I met another woman who does psychological and spiritual healing, she said the same thing: "I see you in a very simple white gown, you're beautiful, you have long curly hair, and you defend people for religious freedom." Then she shook.

"Did you just shake?" I asked her.

"It didn't end very well," she said. Apparently, I was burned at the stake. No joke.

In Palm Springs, when I flipped a card with a snake, the reader asked me a few questions. When I told her about all of the changes I had made the last two years, she just calmly shook her head and said, "You are choosing your cards perfectly." She explained that the snake sheds its skin. "It can't do it quickly, it has to do it in its own time." Just as I had been wishing all the things I was experiencing to happen more quickly so that I could make sense of them all, she explained that I had to be patient, that it was all happening according to plan.

She suggested I read the book *Many Lives, Many Masters* by Dr. Brian Weiss, so I did. That

INSPIRATION | JOHN F. KENNEDY

"THERE ARE RISKS AND COSTS TO ACTION. BUT THEY ARE FAR LESS THAN THE LONG-RANGE RISKS OF COMFORT-ABLE INACTION."

book blew me away. Here was this Harvard-educated psychiatrist who wouldn't have believed in past lives had he not experienced it firsthand while working with a patient under hypnosis. His client was able to see someone in a past life that she knew in her current life, and I realized it was the same experience I've had of meeting someone for the first time and being absolutely certain I've met them before. His descriptions of looking back on life after dying resonated with me as well. How cool would that be to sit on a couch with God, watching your life like a movie? I mean, pass the popcorn! I can see us watching one of my fuck-ups and saying to God, "Oops, I didn't handle that one very well, did I, Boss?" And he'll be like, "Nope. You didn't. And now you'll go back down and learn that lesson again."

According to Dr. Weiss, we meet people who are in our lives to teach us something very specific. They are guides, and they are literally placed in a particular time and place. They are not meant to stay in our lives. They only

EXPLORE

Numerology 101
youtube.com/
watch?v=EL7Ngxpiu28

6 Meanings of
Number 11:11 Decoded
youtube.com/
watch?v=zmi0nDZIChk

arrive to do their job, and then we have to let them go. I've learned so much from the different books I've chosen to read these past few years and this is definitely one of the most essential.

PLAYLIST | STRENGTH

Reach Out
and Touch
Diana Ross

Good Morning
Starshine
(From *The Dish*)
Oliver

Hotel Happiness
Brook Benton

Pennies from
Heaven
Louis Prima

Halo
Beyoncé

Me, Myself & I
**G-Eazy and
Bebe Rexha**

Footprints
Sia

Strength of
a Woman
Mary J. Blige

Landslide
Fleetwood Mac

Danny Boy
Carly Simon

Mahogany
Diana Ross

Past Lives
Børns

People Get Ready
The Impressions

Fighter
Christina Aguilera

Stronger
Kelly Clarkson

Gonna Fly Now
(Theme from *Rocky*)
Bill Conti

Stronger
Britney Spears

Gotta Get
Thru This
Daniel Bedingfield

Glorious
**Macklemore (feat.
Solar Grey)**

Good Vibrations
**Marky Mark and
the Funky Bunch**

This Is Me
(From *The Greatest
Showman*)
Keala Settle

05.

"WHEN DIET IS WRONG, MEDICINE IS OF NO USE. WHEN DIET IS CORRECT, MEDICINE IS OF NO NEED."

AYURVEDA

My Qigong master Beverly once said to me, "Your guardian angels are going to drop people into your life in the
next year."

Sure enough, the next year a girlfriend of mine
introduced me to Sheena Patel, who I now call my
Indian Goddess. She is this gorgeous, young Indian
woman who consults with me by phone now that I
live on the West Coast, motivating me and helping
me to meditate. She only accepts new clients on a
word of mouth basis, so it was synchronistic that
we connected when we did. For over a decade she

EXPLORE

#ayurveda

#skinnyogi

#theayurvedic
experience

has been running a corporate wellness company called Savsani, which provides holistic health solutions to companies, hospitals, and universities. Sheena walked me through mind-body modalities, but maybe more importantly, she also taught me how to nourish my soul through Ayurvedic cooking.

She has taught me so much about Ayurvedic health. She identified my dominant dosha as Pitta, which won't surprise those who know me, and she suggested specific foods for me to eat and stay away from. Dosha is an Ayurvedic medicine device with three energies believed to circulate in the body and to govern physiological activity. The three doshas are Vata, Pitta, and Kapha. Most people have a dominant dosha, or two active doshas with a third less active dosha. You can go online and take a dosha test to see which one you are. Once you've identified your dominant dosha(s), there are a number of resources for how to tailor your diet accordingly.

I understand that many people need prescription drugs, but I try really hard not to go that route. Instead, I try to eat right, exercise, and meditate daily to stay healthy in a more holistic approach. Now that I'm living in California, I feel so in tune to this area of the United States. I recently found a new general practitioner and I'll be damned if after a full physical she didn't give me a cranial massage.

I recently stumbled upon the term "functional medicine" which incorporates both philosophies of Eastern and Western medicine. I've always believed in this, but I'm just beginning to really discover the language for it and truly learn about it. Its main aspects are identifying and treating the root causes of specific diseases, which might be from any number of different issues. Just like many holistic health practices, functional medicine relies heavily on specific diet plans based off of individual needs. I'm so glad to see it's being taken more seriously in the medical industry.

I have made a ton of changes in the past few years, one of the biggest being the food I cook. Having written two cookbooks, I couldn't help but to include some new recipes I've been

EXPLORE

Ayurveda:
The Art of Being
youtube.com/
watch?v=VgJJlceH-vA
Babette's Feast
Chef
Revolution Food
The Hundred-Foot
Journey
Tortilla Soup

tinkering with. I hope you will explore and experiment with Ayurvedic cooking like I have.

My mother was a good cook, and trust me, being married to an Italian guy, she had to be. If she made something my father didn't like, he would say, "Laurie, this is real shit." It's no wonder she finally found the courage to leave him. I worshipped him as a father, but man, he sucked as a husband. He'd go on to say to his six children, "Kids, don't eat this shit. I'll order a pizza for us." During her era there wasn't much experimentation in the kitchen. The grocery stores didn't have the variety of foods they have now, and most housewives who made dinner for their families made pretty simple meals. My mother would always pair the same vegetables with the same meat for the same night of the week. Everything was planned and routine. Now, however, I can walk around my farmers' markets in California and base my meals on what looks good on any given day. I love cooking like that and I'm very grateful that I live in a place where the climate is such that quality fruits and vegetables are available to me all year long.

INSPIRATION | SHIVA SAMHITA

"LET THE YOGI EAT MODERATELY… OTHERWISE, HOWEVER CLEVER, HE CANNOT GAIN SUCCESS."

Here is a letter I received from my friend Sheena, when I told her I was writing this book:

Dear Megan,

I should have known the first time hearing your name wasn't going to be the last since it had to do with my two favorite things: food and bringing people together. Your dearest friend Liz, one of our first Savsani Family members, invited me to your cookbook signing. Somehow, someway, the Universe had its way of bringing us together at the perfect moment.

Soon after, you told me that most people, looking from the outside in, would have thought you had the best life: summers in The Hamptons, memberships to prestigious tennis and golf clubs, three beautiful boys who were grown up and had moved out. Even though life looked great, you expressed to me that you felt like you had been living on auto-pilot for years.

I knew that a way for you to provide more immediate balance to yourself during this transi-

tion was coming back to one of your loves: cooking. Instead of cooking for others, I wanted you to actively engage in cooking for yourself by applying the healing Ayurvedic menu I gave you. It was more than just eating, it was acting in a way to feed your soul again. This allowed us to open up the doors of Sanatana Dharma, begin to unlock your suppressed subconscious, and open you back up to your true self.

Each challenge has its own set of struggles for an individual. You had always expressed a sense of guilt when it came to making the decision to get a divorce and how your sons would be affected. Naturally, as a mother, you worry about your children's well-being no matter how old they are. Remember that you have an infinite amount of love to supply to them and they will always carry that throughout the rest of their lives, just as Bhumi's (Mother Earth's) nature is to provide us with plentiful fruits and vegetables even after we toil and dig at her. You have opened up to what is important to yourself, not money and things, but to live in love and to share that love with the world. In this "reproductive stage", it's about sharing yourself truthfully with the world. After digging around, we found your inner voice so you can express yourself. That's why I mentioned you should consider writing a book because I knew that it would not only help you but also help others on this journey of life.

I remember writing this note to you towards the beginning of our journey together, and it hasn't changed a bit:

> "As each moment goes by, affirmations for yourself move you in a positive direction forward. As your journey is like a river on a natural course to the vast and infinite ocean, you will know the right direction at the right time. You know what you need to do and where you need to be. Open to the Universe and remember that YOU ARE WORTH IT! You are full and complete and there is nothing to fear. Om."

Sincerely,
Sheena

EXPLORE | DOSHA QUIZ

These questions are designed just to help you understand the science of Ayurveda. In Ayurveda no body, no temperament, no person is exactly the same. With this in mind Ayurvedic doctors help you to better pinpoint where you fall along the dosha spectrum to better help you live a long and healthy life. This short quiz will help you understand that there are three different types of doshas. If you want to know more about yourself schedule an appointment with an Ayurvedic practitioner in your area. Even better, take a trip to India and make an appointment with an Ayurvedic doctor— they are part of the health care system there and even in the spas. They will be able to guide you deeper and further. If you have any questions about recommendations on where to go, please contact sheena@savsani.com.

DOSHA QUIZ (circle one)

Body Size: small / medium / large

Tone: bony / athletic / muscular

Skin: dry / sensitive / oily

Climate: dry / humid / cold

Hands/Feet: cold / neutral / warm

Sleep: light / medium / deep

Stamina: exhausted / strong / long

Focus: changeable / bright / driven

Memory: short term / forgetful / long term

Temperament: quick / hyper / relaxed

Results: More answers on the left is Vata; more answers in the middle is Pitta; more answers on the right is Kapha.

Recipes

I couldn't write a book without putting some recipes in it. Friends and family have enjoyed my first two cookbooks, and with the new me and all the changes that I've made in my life, I find I cook differently. I wanted to share just a few super healthy recipes that I hope you will try and enjoy.

Most of these new recipes were inspired by my friend Sheena, who has taught me a lot. My pantry and refrigerator are full of new and exciting food items that I have never bought before in my life. For instance, I now put cinnamon in breakfast foods and smoothies because it is loaded with anti-oxidants, which protect the body from oxidative damage caused by free radicals. I have also learned to use turmeric more. It's a wonderful anti-inflammatory spice, and since I wake up in pain every morning I need as much turmeric as I can stomach. I've seen huge differences in my recovery times after tough workouts ever since I started incorporating turmeric into my diet.

Recipes Sheena created were

EXPLORE

Ayurveda Cooking
for Beginners
Laura Plumb

Eat Feel Fresh
Sahara Rose Ketabi

120

EXPLORE

Ayurveda Over
Western Medicines
with Dr. B.M Hegde,
TEDxMITE
youtube.com/watch?
v=HzTvEK1sVi0

Introduction
to Ayurveda
youtube.com/watch?
v=EV7B5-6qQQc

to help pacify my elevated Pitta levels. These levels had increased because of the stress I was under during the changes I was going through at the time. The recipes below, however, will work for all doshas, so anyone can begin incorporating them to eat more like a yogi. This means eating whole foods that come straight from the earth: vegetables, fruits, legumes, nuts, and seeds. And greens, greens, greens. My suggestion is to eat greens with every meal. I learned that once you become conscious of how you eat, and what affects you, you notice your mind will gradually open and you will come to fully realize all the divinity around you.

It has been a fun journey this year, and I owe so much to Sheena, my Indian Goddess!

EXPLORE

Savasani
savsani.com

Functional Medicine
ifm.org/functional-
medicine/what-is-func-
tional-medicine/

Dosha Quiz
shop.chopra.com/
dosha-quiz

Ayurveda Class
dailyom.com/cgi-bin/
display/articledisplay.
cgi?aid=67180

Breakfast

RED QUINOA with YOGURT

Quinoa is gluten free and high in protein. It's also a good source of fiber and magnesium. I use it now instead of rice, and I really like the nutty taste. Here I use it for a breakfast item, but it's also great under vegetables for lunch and dinner.

Serves: 1

1 cup of red quinoa (cook as directed on package)*

½ cup of yogurt (whatever flavor you choose)**

1 teaspoon of pre-soaked chia seeds

1 orange, grated using microplane, plus juice of ½ orange

½ cup of blueberries

drizzle of honey on top or cinnamon (optional)

To serve, place a portion of the cooked red quinoa in a bowl. Place yogurt on top, then a dollop of chia seeds, grated orange, squeezed juice of half of the orange, place blueberries on top, and if you like, drizzle honey or sprinkle cinnamon on top.

* Keep extra red quinoa for another day.

** If I see freshly made ricotta cheese, I'll substitute it for yogurt for a real treat. After all, my maiden name is Silletti!

Breakfast

CHIA SEED PUDDING

Chia seeds are a superfood and really, really good for you, but you digest them better if they are pre-soaked. They are also a great source of fiber and protein. I put 1 cup of chia seeds in a plastic container with 2 cups of water and keep in my refrigerator to add to smoothies.

Here is a recipe for Chia Seed Pudding, but as you can see you can make this awesome breakfast any way you like. Be creative and experiment. It's also a great breakfast to take on-the-go because you can store it in a covered container that you can take with you.

Serves: 2

½ cup of chia seeds
2 cups of unsweetened almond, cashew, or hemp milk
drizzle of vanilla extract
drizzle of maple syrup
berries for topping
cinnamon, nuts, coconut flakes, and/or pumpkin seeds
(all optional)

1. Blend chia seeds with milk, vanilla extract, and maple syrup in a covered container. Cover tightly and shake it.

2. Place container in refrigerator overnight.

3. Shake again the next morning before opening.

To serve, spoon a serving into a bowl and get creative. Place whatever you like on top. Add berries, sprinkle cinnamon, if you like walnuts or almonds you could crush and sprinkle those on top. Add coconut flakes or seeds, too.

If you want this on-the-go, pour your chia seed mixture into a few covered containers and follow the same directions.

I use chocolate flavored sometimes—it's also delicious!

Breakfast

BLUEBERRY SMOOTHIE

Blueberries are so good for you. They are low in calories and high in fiber, vitamin C, and vitamin K. They are also the king of antioxidants. (But be sure to check your teeth in the mirror as blueberries stuck on a tooth are as bad as spinach or lettuce. And please be the friend who tells me when I have something stuck in my teeth!)

Makes: 2-3 tall glasses

- **1** cup or 6 ounces of fresh blueberries
- **½** avocado
- **1** tablespoon of pre-soaked chia seeds
- **1** tablespoon of apple cider vinegar
- **1½** cups of chocolate or vanilla coconut water, hemp milk, or rice milk
- **1** scoop of chocolate or vanilla protein powder (vegetable-based)
- **1** tablespoon of super collagen powder or Sun Potion's Mucuna Pruriens powder
- **1** cup of crushed ice

Place all contents in a blender and blend until smooth. If too thick add some water or more liquid.

Breakfast

PRUNE SMOOTHIE
(This ought to get your pipes moving!)
Makes: 2-3 tall glasses

10 Prunes (pre-soaked in ½ cup of water for 5 minutes)
1 tablespoon of pre-soaked chia seeds
2 cups of chocolate or vanilla coconut water,
hemp milk, or rice milk
1 scoop of chocolate or vanilla protein powder
(vegetable-based)
1 tablespoon of super collagen powder or
Sun Potion's Mucuna Pruriens powder
pinch of cinnamon
1 cup of crushed ice

Place all contents in a blender and blend until smooth.
If too thick add some water or more liquid.

Breakfast

SPINACH and EGGS

I learned this from my fantastic daughter-in-law Maggie who comes from a healthy and culinarily exploratory family. I love talking with my son as he cooks in their kitchen. He sounds just like my father when he describes food, which warms my heart.

Serves: 2

- **1** tablespoon of butter
- **1** shallot, chopped (1 tablespoon or more to taste)
- **3** mushroom caps, sliced
- **2** cups of fresh spinach, rinsed well˙
- **2** eggs
  Freshly ground pepper
  Pink Himalayan sea salt grounded or Kosher salt

1. In a sauté pan, place butter, shallots, and mushrooms and sauté approximately 3 to 5 minutes.
2. Add spinach to sauté pan and sauté on medium heat until soft, approximately 3 minutes.
3. Break 2 eggs on top of spinach and cover pot. Turn heat off. Should only take about 3 minutes to cook.
4. Add salt and pepper to taste.
˙Could substitute kale or cooked lentils.

Soup

CAULIFLOWER SOUP

The kitchen smells so beautiful while this is cooking. It can also make a wonderful dip. I place it in a bowl and surround it with brightly colored vegetables for a crudité. You'll be a hit when you bring this to your next book club meeting or Super Bowl party.

Serves: 4

- **1** teaspoon of olive oil
- **1** cup of onion, chopped
- **¼** teaspoon of fennel seeds
- **2** teaspoons of shredded coconut (optional)
- **1** teaspoon of coriander powder
     pinch of turmeric
- **1** cauliflower, chopped (roughly 2-3 cups)
     a pinch of Himalayan sea salt or Kosher salt
- **1** 13.5-ounce can of coconut milk

1. Heat oil in a medium pot.

2. Add onions, fennel seeds, and coconut (if using) and sauté for approximately 3 minutes.

3. Add spices and let toast for approximately 2 minutes.

4. Add cauliflower and salt to the pot. Stir and cook for approximately 4 to 5 minutes until blended.

5. Pour in milk, cover, and cook on medium heat for 20 minutes until cauliflower is soft.

6. Let soup cool a bit before pulsing with a hand blender or regular blender until smooth. Adjust texture by adding more coconut milk if necessary.

Dinner

CHICKPEA CURRY

Chickpeas are the same as garbanzo beans. Apparently Middle Easterners call them chickpeas, but in the States they are called garbanzo beans. I love this dish not only because it's healthy but also because it gets better each day like soups do. I eat it by itself, or as a side dish with fish or chicken for those of us who are not vegetarian. You can also serve it over rice or red quinoa for a hearty dish.

Serves: 4

- **2** teaspoons of olive oil
- **1** cup of yellow onion, chopped

3 cloves of garlic, chopped
½ inch of ginger, grated or finely chopped
1 green chili pepper or jalapeño, grated or finely chopped
pinch of Kosher salt
½ teaspoon of garam masala
½ teaspoon of turmeric
½ teaspoon of smoked paprika
pinch of ground cloves
1 cup of puréed crushed tomatoes
1 can of chickpeas, rinsed
squeeze of lime to taste
parsley, chopped for garnish

1. In a medium saucepan, heat oil on medium heat.

2. Add onions, garlic, ginger, chili pepper, and salt to pot and cook until translucent for approximately 5 minutes.

3. Add spices, stir to combine, and cook another 3 minutes.

4. Add tomatoes, stir to combine, and cover for 10 minutes.

5. Add chickpeas, stir to combine, and cook uncovered for 5 minutes.

6. Add lime to taste and chopped parsley for garnish.

"AYURVEDA IS A SISTER PHILOSOPHY TO YOGA. IT IS THE SCIENCE OF LIFE OR LONGEVITY AND IT TEACHES ABOUT THE POWER AND THE CYCLES OF NATURE, AS WELL AS THE ELEMENTS."

Dinner

TOFU with TOASTED SESAME SEEDS

I never thought I'd be a tofu eating sort of chick, but Sheena has turned me onto some tofu dishes that I actually like. This one in particular is fantastic. It's perfect as a first course, at a party on a tray with toothpicks, or as a nice lunch or side dish.

Serves: 2

- **2** tablespoons of sesame seeds
- **2** tabelspoons of sesame oil
- ½ cup of firm organic tofu, dried with a paper towel, then cut into 1-inch cubes
- **2** tablespoons of Bragg Liquid Aminos

1. In a sauté pan on medium heat, toast sesame seeds in sesame oil.

2. Add tofu to sauté pan and stir-fry for approximately 2 minutes, occasionally turning the tofu to brown sides.

3. Add Bragg Liquid Aminos and toss to cover tofu. Immediately turn heat off.

Serve warm and enjoy this healthy, beautiful dish.

Dinner

MASOOR DAL
(Spiced Red Lentils)

Serves: 2

- ½ cup of masoor dal (red lentils)
- **2** cups of water
  pinch of Kosher salt
- **3** teaspoons of ghee
- ¼ teaspoon of ground turmeric
- ½ teaspoon of ground cumin
- ¼ teaspoon of garam masala
- **3** cloves of garlic, minced
- **1** medium tomato, chopped
- **1** red onion, chopped
- **1** cup of cilantro, chopped for garnish
- ½ lime, squeezed
- **1** avocado, diced (optional)

1. Wash and drain the masoor dal.

2. In a medium pot, add dal, water, and salt. Cook on medium heat for 10 minutes. Be careful not to overcook.

3. In another saucepan, add ghee, turmeric,

cumin, garam masala, and garlic. Sauté for approximately 3 minutes or until golden.

4. Add tomato, then onions. Cook until translucent, approximately 5 more minutes.

5. Spoon dal in individual bowls, top with tomato and onion mixture.

Top with chopped cilantro and avocado (if using). Add a squeeze of lime. Serve warm.

Fresh turmeric is amazing if you are lucky enough to find it. It's an anti-inflammatory spice that I use whenever I can—I sprinkle it on nearly everything except my toothbrush! It's a root, much like fresh ginger, and needs to be peeled before chopping. Obviously, ground turmeric is easier and more accessible.

EXPLORE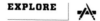

Jiva VPK Test Ayurveda
with Steven Rudolph

EXPLORE

Ayurveda for
Natural Healing

PLAYLIST | HARMONY

Unstoppable
Sia

Think
Aretha Franklin

Rise Up
Audra Day

Mama Said
Lukas Graham

Take the World
by Storm
Lukas Graham

The Climb
Miley Cyrus

Somebody to Love
Jefferson Airplane

What a
Wonderful World
Louis Armstrong

Breakaway
Kelly Clarkson

There's Nothing
Holdin' Me Back
Shawn Mendes

I Will Survive
Gloria Gaynor

Survivor
Destiny's Child

Chariots of Fire
(The Main Theme)
Vangelis

Gravity
Tim McGraw

Keep on Truckin'
Eddie Kendricks

Legendary
Welshly Arms

Be Cool,
Be Calm
Stevie Wonder

My Way
Frank Sinatra

We Are Family
Sister Sledge

Turn! Turn! Turn!
The Byrds

06.

"WHAT NINE MONTHS OF ATTEN- TION DOES FOR AN EMBRYO, FORTY EARLY MORNINGS ALONE WILL DO FOR YOUR GRAD- UALLY GROWING WHOLENESS."

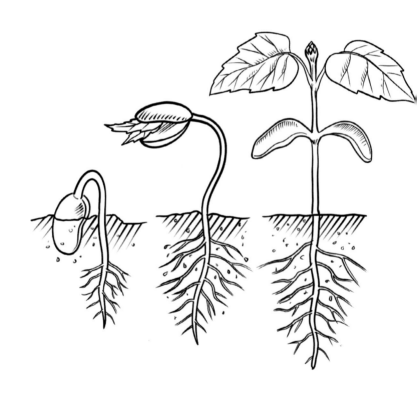

RITUALS

In 2016, I was fifty-six years old and living alone for the first time in an apartment in Boston. It's strange to write that sentence, but it's true. After separating from my husband of thirty-three years, it was a huge adjustment.

In the very beginning, I created daily rituals that brought order to my day. If you're looking to kick-start a new discipline in your life, or you're struggling to change a habit, I highly recommend establishing a few daily rituals that you observe no matter what. You might like to try what worked for me or you might come up with things that work better for you, but I suggest creating realistic routines and sticking with them. By doing so, you will have multiple anchors to steady you throughout your day, develop a sense of accomplishment after completing rituals no matter how small, and experience an inner calmness and new meaning in your life.

One ritual that I didn't actively seek out, but that found me, was receiving daily phone calls from my dear friend Lydia. I didn't even realize how badly I needed those calls and that regularity. She was always checking on me and giving me TLC. I'm so blessed and grateful that I have her in my life. What a gift.

During this phase, my Qigong master told me, "Your angels are very excited about your 'growth spurt'. For them, it's like a gardener's happiness when their flowers start to bloom. Your soul is trying to bloom. You need to find out who and what you really are and what will bring you joy and satisfaction. Your soul is so beautiful, it is sunshine, grass, and flowers. Your job is to keep feeding it, watering it, and letting 'Little Sprout' grow!"

So, after trying just about everything under the sun these past two years, here is what I've settled on and incorporated into my daily life:

1

TEA AND PRAYERS

I make a cup of herbal tea first thing in the morning. Even the smell of it brings a calmness to me. I was a devoted Italian roast, two cups a morning kind of girl, but now I treat myself to coffee only on weekends, when I enjoy walking my new puppy, Paco, to a local coffee shop. Truth be told, I'm so excited about that weekend cup of coffee that we basically jog there!

Early on in this journey, when I was still living in Boston, I would light a candle, sit in a comfortable chair near my statue of Mary, and begin my morning prayers while drinking my tea. Now that I'm living in sunny California, I don't need to light a candle because it's so gloriously sunny here, but I still do my prayers. Having been raised Catholic, I still find comfort in saying an Our Father and a Hail Mary. It's interesting that in some religions there is the holding of beads like in the Catholic faith. I also think the repetition of prayers is like a form of meditation as it helps create a breathing pattern that is soothing. I then start a conversation with God and Mary. I thank them for a few things like my health and the health of my three sons, I thank them

EXPLORE

Habit Hub:
Routine & Habits

Coach.me

Sleep Cycle

for being surrounded by so many loving family members and friends, and I usually add being thankful for something in nature like a beautiful sky or the ocean. I also ask them to help family and friends who are hurting either physically or mentally. Then I begin my long list of things I want...

You see, I've "hired" an army of angels to help me. Let me explain: when I was thinking of moving to California and making trips to look at real estate, I stumbled upon a woman in the Aura Shop in Venice Beach. Her name was Nicole, and I instantly had a connection with her. It was no surprise to me that she was born in New Jersey (I always gravitate towards people from my home state). I was so looking forward to spending more time with her when I moved to Santa Monica. Unfortunately, shortly after I did, I learned she had died suddenly of cancer. I was heartbroken. I loved following her Instagram which was filled with motivational sayings with unicorns and sparkles. One of the many things I have learned is that sometimes people are brought to you as guides or teachers. It's a really beautiful thing. I'm so lucky these guides are sent to me exactly when I need them, and sometimes they only stick around to teach one specific lesson before leaving. I'm truly blessed. Anyway, Nicole suggested a book for me to read which was *Hiring the Heavens* by Jean Slatter. In it, she suggests creating a personal army of angels to pray to. I gave it a lot of thought and I came up with my army. Of course, I included God and Mary, but then I thought, Archangel Michael is such a badass, he's the one with a shield and is a warrior, who wouldn't want him on their team? I included my closest ancestors, too: my mother, my father, my maternal grandparents Poppy and Grandma, who lived with us when I was growing up, and I added Zak, my youngest son's friend who had recently passed away, because I knew he would be willing to help me. After I heard the sad news of Nicole's death and after my beloved brother Johnnie died, I added them to my army as well.

Early on, my prayers were:

1. To help my divorce pass quickly and with grace.
2. That my three sons always love and respect me.
3. To understand God's will for me.

"A DAILY RITUAL IS A WAY OF SAYING I'M VOTING FOR MYSELF, I'M TAKING CARE OF MYSELF."

I've also learned that God has a plan for each of us. We are basically born with a blueprint. All my life I was a relentless goal setter. I would decide what I wanted, figure out what steps needed to be done to reach it, and I would work diligently towards achieving my goal. Now that I've gotten older and wiser, I give it up to God. I might ask for something but then I let it go to the universe. Sure, I always want my wishes to come quickly, but I've learned I can pray for it, think positive thoughts, and then ultimately let it go and hope for the best! I'm told that sometimes you get more than you actually wanted if you just "Let It Be". I heard an interview with Paul McCartney where he talked about the inspiration for that song. He was at a crossroad in his life and his mother had just passed away. During a dream, she appeared to him and said those words. When he woke up, he sat down and wrote that song.

2

MEDITATION

After my prayers, when I have finished my tea, I then try to meditate for about fifteen to twenty minutes.

I say try because, as I explain in the chapter on Meditation, I have found it to be quite difficult. Regardless of how well it goes each day, I have to remind myself that it's called a meditation "practice" for a reason, and I try to give myself a break on the days that don't seem as successful as others.

EXPLORE

Beautiful candles
lafco.com

Daily affirmations
louisehay.com/
affirmations/

East Coast
Herbal Clinic
commonwealth
herbs.com

West Coast
Herbal Store
dragonherbs.com

3

INTENTIONS

After prayer and meditation, I sit and think about what intentions I would like to set for my day. I'm finding that when I set an intention for the day, I'll be damned if it doesn't appear. For instance, I might decide that it should be playfulness and I'll find myself eating lunch at a table near a playground watching children laugh and play. Or, on days when I make my intention to experience gratitude and end up noticing a magnificent tree that I pass all the time, I realize how lucky I am to have such a deep connection to natural beauty. This is something Johnnie would often do while we walked, and in that way, he's still very much here, teaching me how to be present and live in the moment.

4

AFFIRMATIONS

I'm learning so many new techniques this year which have helped me to gain confidence and accept all of the changes in my life. Saying affirmations out loud is all about helping to change your thinking. People who see the cup half-full versus those who see it half-empty lead healthier lives, and by using affirmations regularly, we have a much better chance of being in the half-full crowd. The moment you set affirmations you are stepping out of the role of victim. You are no longer helpless. You are acknowledging your own power.

Here are a few examples:

- I am focused on the positive possibilities of my future life.
- Wow, that was an interesting time in my life. What an amazing chapter.

- I am confident, loving, and happy.
- Unknown and unexpected good is coming my way today.

It's about being positive. It's like the movie *Field of Dreams* with the gorgeous Kevin Costner, when a voice tells him, "If you build it, they will come." Or, one of my favorite words of wisdom from my father that I literally live by is, "Dreams are for free, Babe, so you might as well dream big!" Anybody who knows me knows that I dream big, but then I work hard towards making them come true. Positive thinking and putting in the work can make all your dreams come true.

I happened to find a box of "Butterfly Affirmations" in a little gift shop while visiting Beverly in Durango, Colorado. Each morning I pick a card out of this box and enjoy reading the positive statements. Today's was, "The love within me is more powerful than doubt or fear." I know for a fact that before leaving Boston I was operating out of doubt and fear. No one wants to be with

EXPLORE |

#howtomanifest

#affirmations

#theuniversehas yourback

#soupersoul

#eckharttolle

#bereal

#rumi_poetry

someone who is doing that. I promise you, if you incorporate even one habit that I've suggested, you too will feel better. I now can say that I'm on my way to becoming happier and healthier in mind, body, and spirit than I've ever been.

5

HOROSCOPE

Of course a chick like me is going to read her horoscope each day. Matter of fact, I read all three. I can't help myself. I'm a Virgo with Cancer rising and my moon is in Gemini—pretty perfect combo if you ask me. Virgos love order and home is important to them, Cancers are warm and kind, and Geminis are good communicators. I was told recently by Chris Flisher, who does my astrological chart, that as you get older your rising sign becomes significant.

I still love the story of my birth, which comes to me occasionally when I'm reading my daily horoscope. My mother was a pretty lady. She was well-dressed (on a budget) and well-kempt. There were six of us total, and I was the oldest of the bottom three, so my father called me the captain of the JV team. My mother was so excited after a four-year break to have me. She started to go into labor and decided she needed to paint her toenails. (How fantastic?!) She was Irish, and everyone knows they are the best storytellers. I can see her now telling the story. She said, "I put my hair in a ponytail and started to paint my toes when all of a sudden I felt this pain and threw the nail polish bottle across the goddamn room! Then I realized I forgot to call your father." I always laughed at that. When she finally called him, he was at the bar he owned in Hoboken, and he asked a friend who was a cop to meet him at our apartment. I was taken to the hospital with a police escort—siren, lights, and all! C'mon, that's like movie star stuff.

There are so many parallels in my own life with my mother's life, it's creepy. When I was pregnant with my Gregory, I, too, was painting my nails while in the maternity ward. I was hooked up to an IV with Pitocin which was supposed to encourage my little dancer to "come on down" as they used to say on *The Price is Right*. A nurse entered the room to check on me and I said, "You know, I think I'm having a contraction." She responded, in a thick Boston

"THERE ARE THREE SOLUTIONS TO EVERY PROBLEM: ACCEPT IT, CHANGE IT, OR LEAVE IT. IF YOU CAN'T ACCEPT IT, CHANGE IT. IF YOU CAN'T CHANGE IT, LEAVE IT."

accent, "Honey, if you were having a contraction that bottle of nail polish would be flying across the room right about now." As she was walking out of the room, she said nonchalantly, "Oh, by the way, leave your pinky unpolished because we need to know you are getting enough oxygen."

6

SPIRITUAL READING

My sister and her partner sent me a subscription for *Daily Word*, a daily inspiration for unity. It's a spiritual website that I enjoy reading the second I wake up. For instance, today's reading was, "Freedom: I work and live free in Spirit." It gives just a few centering thoughts for my day. Here was another great one:

> *"Renewal: I am renewed in spirit, ready to begin again. Becoming aware of my ability and power to change thoughts, perspectives, and habits is the beginning of a renewal process. I consciously observe my thought patterns and seek to reevaluate any beliefs*

152

contrary to my well-being and divine poten-
tial. I make a renewed commitment to self-
care and to provide my body with adequate
rest, nourishment, and encouragement. My
whole being responds in kind."

And one final sentence that resonates with me, because I love being out in nature: "Just as new growth sprouts forth from trees after dormancy, I am renewed, ready to begin again." Boo-yah! Or, as Emeril used to say on his cooking show, "Bam!"

I subscribe to DailyOM by Madisyn Taylor, who wrote an excellent book by the same name. My copy nearly glows in the dark I've highlighted so many lines. Each morning, they email wonderful inspirational topics to ponder that help you think positively and prevent negative thoughts or negative people from entering your energy field. I've learned a lot from this website. Today's topic was: "Falling in Love with Yourself: Once you discover how to fall in love with yourself, you can't help but treat yourself with respect and thoughtfulness. It's all about the magic of your intentions and the power of your actions."

7

DREAM JOURNAL

I've been keeping a dream journal for a few years now and it's fascinating watching it evolve. When I started this on March 15, 2017, I often dreamed I was in some form of transportation and always in the passenger seat. If I remember a dream in the morning, then I quickly either write it down or get to my computer and type it out before I forget it. Eventually, I found myself not in the passenger seats of cars, planes, and trains, but walking on my own two feet on a pathway leading people who were behind me.

Our mind rehashes things from our day while we are sleeping and sorts things out, if you will. Sometimes I wake up with ideas for my book. Other times, a loved one who has passed away shows up, and I wake up with this lovely sense of calm. Because I'm a type-A person, I even use ALL CAPS for colors in my dream journal. I told this to a dream specialist and she was very impressed. She said she's never had a client who's done that. Must be a Virgo thing!

Here are a few entries from my dream journal:

EXPLORE

Chariots of Fire
Chef's Table
Season 3, Episode 1:
Jeong Kwan
Field of Dreams
Rocky
Rudy

6/27/17 *Dreamed last night I was in a CAR in front right-side passenger seat on a highway. We wanted to go off the exit but we must have been too far right. A biker—not motorcycle—was on my right. Big muscle guy. (Perhaps my guardian angel?) He wouldn't let us turn off that exit. We would have hit him I suppose. I was apologizing to him. But he stayed really close to my window. We were going very slow and it was like he was guiding the CAR to bear left and to not take that exit to the right.*

10/31/17 *DRIVING on a highway—got lost—went to a library. Woman gave me a GOLD xmas tree ornament in shape of a DOVE.*

1/31/18 *I was LEADING a group on FOOT along a dirt path heading into a beautiful GREEN forest. A gentle hike—a "walk in the woods". I felt calm and in control!!!!!*

INSPIRATION | BUDDHA, ON FORGIVENESS

"HOLDING TO ANGER IS LIKE GRASPING A HOT COAL WITH THE INTENT OF THROWING IT AT SOMEONE ELSE. YOU ARE THE ONE WHO GETS BURNED."

8

PERSONAL JOURNAL

I have been keeping a personal journal for over twenty years. I find such solace in writing. My friend and life coach, Perry, suggested I read *The Artist's Way* by Julia Cameron. The author encourages readers to handwrite three pages of their thoughts each morning and explains how helpful that can be. Perry gave me the coolest journal, which I filled up quickly. I also type it out at times. I love going back and reading my entries from years ago. I've been told so many times by these spiritual people I've been going to how intuitive I am and that I should always follow my intuitions. I'm not so sure I felt that I was, but one day while reading an entry in my journal going back to the early '90s, I stumbled upon something that really stopped me in my tracks. I wrote that I didn't think it was good for my marriage to be getting all dressed up to attend events with hundreds of people only to barely talk to my husband all night. When couples I know get married, I write all of them a personal letter with some "old lady" or "sage" advice. And the two things I am adamant

EXPLORE

Morning Rituals of
Tony Robbins, Oprah,
Steve Jobs, Lady
Gaga and the Most
Successful People
youtube.com/watch?
v=Xb02qGHngb0

about for a good marriage are: date night and communication.

Below is just one entry from my personal journal that I'm so deeply glad I recorded. It was such a profound day and meeting, and I don't think I would have remembered the maternal connections I made if I'd waited until after I returned to the States to write it down. Capturing how I experienced something meaningful on the day I actually experienced it, I can now revisit that day and know exactly what I was feeling at that moment in time. What a gift we give ourselves when we journal.

> **5/18/17** *Had a life-changing experience today. Thank you, God. I've been praying daily to find peace of mind, asking him and Mary to help me. Some days I ask for my mother to come because on days when I do feel her presence I'm happiest. I start each day with prayers and state my "intentions for the day". Today (and often) mine was "Gratitude".*

Originally I did not choose to go to the Jinkwan Temple from the itinerary, but Rob, who I sent the choices to, suggested very strongly that I NOT miss that. I'm so so grateful he did as it was MINDBLOWING—

From the second we stepped off the bus we were greeted by this amazing monk named Soon Woo. The moment she began to talk with us I felt this overwhelming feeling—this energy—of love and compassion. She told us before hiking up the mountain to the temple to look up at the sky, then notice the trees, to smell the air and to ENJOY. She kept smiling and used the word ENJOY at least 30 times. I felt a connection to her so I found myself walking very close to her.

Then, after reaching the temple and taking off my shoes to embark on the best cooking class I have ever taken (and I've taken many around the world), I met the head chef, the monk named Kae Ho. Again, I felt an incredible connection to this woman. She kept

159

holding my hand. I wanted to be next to her the whole time. I almost tear up writing this because I felt this truly overwhelming feeling being next to her. Could God have sent me my mother today? While I sat next to her to eat what she made for us, she kept reaching for the food and serving me. I observed how she ate each dish and the order in which she ate and I learned and followed her like a child learns from a mother through observation. She didn't speak a word of English, but we totally communicated through food and compassion.

At one point, she even sang to us. I felt like a loved child. I really needed this. Then, as I was putting my shoes back on to leave, she came to me and grabbed my hand to bring me back into the temple. I didn't understand why but I just followed her. As it turns out, there was a TV crew filming a documentary on "temple food" and Kae Ho wanted me to be interviewed. I begged her to hold my hand while they asked me questions, but she

*refused—she didn't want the cameras on her—
God, this woman was so cool. I have a video of
what I said—I hope I said the right things—I
was so honored to have had this experience.*

*On our way to the tea ceremony I stayed very
close to Soon Woo. I shared with her my fear
of telling my children when I returned that
me and their father were getting divorced.
She was so compassionate. During her
presentation, she kept looking right at me,
basically talking to me. I kept my camera
on "video" and I hope I captured a lot of
what she was saying as she was so smart
(working on her PhD), kind, and enlight-
ened. The most important thing she said
is, "Don't regret your past, don't fear your
future—just focus on NOW—on today—and
ENJOY—SMILE."*

*When we returned to the hotel I ran to my
room to sign both of my books (I had a
feeling I should bring a few), and the bus
driver from our tour who smiled at me said*

INSPIRATION | UNKNOWN

"DEAR SOUL: I'M STILL LEARNING ABOUT WHAT YOU LOVE. I'M GOING TO GIVE US MORE OF THAT. I PROMISE."

he would "be honored" to bring them to the
monks. I'm so happy I could share that with
them. Soon Woo kept saying how wonderful
it was that I had written 2 cookbooks—she
was special—Kae Ho was special—I totally
felt grateful. Namaste.

9
EXERCISE

I'm a huge believer in physical exercise, so four to five days a week I do cardio, sit-ups, and lift weights. I then go for a long walk with my puppy. I also love to play tennis, so I try to do that as often as I can, and I take yoga classes regularly.

As you can see, I spend a lot of time getting ready to face my day. I'm laughing my ass off as I write

EXPLORE | EXERCISE

Get physical. Join a gym if you can; park your car as far away as possible to entrances; climb stairs if you can instead of taking elevators; go for walks; take a yoga class; learn to play tennis or any sport; take a hike; go for a bike ride—if you don't own one, rent one. It's so fun to ride a bike along Venice Beach here in Southern California!

this because people will probably think it has to be around 4:00 p.m. when I'm done with all of this stuff! It really isn't that bad, and I do wake up early which helps a lot. And that's just my morning ritual—I have an evening ritual as well!

Evenings

1

YOGA

I always sleep better when I take a yoga class at night. I took up yoga as part of this journey. Whenever I took classes before, I would either get bored quickly or my competitiveness would try to get me to where others were, but being really tight I would just end up getting hurt. Now, taking classes in California, I've come to love the tenderness and compassion the instructors show towards the classes they teach. Plus, the bodies of these yogis are sick, and they are all ages, which really inspires me.

2

HOT BATH

Taking hot baths in Himalayan pink sea salts with some almond oil does wonders for me. I like to work out, but there is always some part of my body that hurts at the end of the day. Himalayan pink sea salts release toxins and help relieve sore muscles. Occasionally I'll add ylang ylang or another essential oil for a true aromatherapy experience. I buy bushels of Himalayan sea salt from Amazon. You can also easily buy Epsom salt from CVS. They make them now in lavender and eucalyptus. Another favorite of mine is Dr. Singh Mustard Seed bath salts. This stuff is good shit, man! My body feels warm all over thirty minutes after I get out of the bath. Lighting a candle is always a good idea, too. Some nights I literally don't turn the lights on in my bathroom—I'm a bit of a kook really. I sometimes brush my teeth in the dark—a real nut job, I tell you! Taking a bath is not meditation, but I can almost guarantee that if you try meditating ten to twenty minutes each morning and end your day with

EXPLORE

Happiness Spells:
5 Minute Lists of
Happy Things

Life Kit from NPR

The Tony
Robbins Podcast

yoga and a bath, those of you who take pills to help you sleep may, and I say may, not need to. It sure is more cost effective buying a bag of Epsom salt at CVS. Just think, if you are lucky enough to crawl into bed after implementing some of these daily routines as a relaxed and happy person with someone who loves you and who you love in return, then chances are you

SHOPPING LIST | RITUALS

Buy yourself some nice herbal teas. Chamomile or Mint are lovely but see what you like. Turmeric tea with black pepper is great for anti-inflammatory purposes. If you are lucky enough to have what I have here in California, which are herbal shops, you can literally discuss any ailment and they will make suggestions for you specifically.

Buy some beautiful aromatic candles of scents that relax you.

Buy a box of affirmation cards. I love the Butterfly Collection—blueangelonline.com/butterfly_affirmations.html.

Buy some journals that make you happy. Even Staples carries some from Martha Stewart!

Buy some nice pens, too. I find there is something special about writing in a journal by hand with a special pen.

Buy either Pink Himalayan sea salt or Epsom salt, available on Amazon.

Buy Dr. Singh Mustard Seed Bath Salts, available on Amazon.

Get a library card, and join Hoopla and Kanopy to watch movies for free.

are going to bed happy and waking up happy. If we were all less stressed and waking up having sex (yep, she went there!), we would all be saying Namaste to everyone we pass on the sidewalk!

3

GRATITUDE JOURNAL

I don't let a night go by where I don't write a few lines in my gratitude journal. You would be surprised if you don't already do this that no matter how bad your day is you can always find a few things you are grateful for. There is scientific research about the health benefits of people who regularly practice acts of gratitude. Those are the people who see the cup as half-full, and statistics show they actually live longer. I'm not surprised by this. If you are happier, you are healthier. I have been doing this for about eight years now and I love reading my entries. I say it all of the time, "I am so blessed with so many loving people in my life." My gratitude journal is full of examples of people being there for me. I also often mention nature. Now that I'm living in California, I'm eternally grateful for the sunshine. Today, as I'm working on this part of the book, my family and friends back East are sending me photos of yet another snowstorm. Yuck! I don't miss that at all. I don't see myself ever moving back to the Northeast.

4
FORGIVENESS

Along with gratitude, forgiveness has been the other thing I've been working at practicing regularly this year. Remember that forgiveness is for you, not necessarily for the other person. I know forgiveness is a lot harder than gratitude, but it's equally important. In my butterfly box of daily intentions, I stumbled upon this one that I love: "Forgiveness helps me

---

EXPLORE | FORGIVENESS

Try a forgiveness exercise. Write down on a piece of paper what someone did or said to you that hurt you. Then, light it on fire. Toss it into a body of water if you can (I've used my kitchen sink during a Boston winter). The concept is that you are using all of your senses—feeling the pen while writing, smelling the fire, seeing it go into flames, and even hearing it singe when it hits the water. It's a release of any emotions attached to that person or thing that they did that hurt you.

to let go and move on with my life, opening up to new and loving experiences."

Another important lesson I learned along my journey is to forgive myself. I don't know if you are like me, but I sometimes beat the crap out of myself. Everyone who knows me knows I'm an Instagram whore. I follow a lot of inspiring Instagrams, and today, Gabrielle Bernstein, a superstar and author in the mindfulness field, posted the following: "Forgive yourself for not knowing better at the time. Forgive yourself for giving away your power. Forgive yourself for past behaviors. Forgive yourself for the survival patterns and traits that you picked up while enduring trauma. Forgive yourself for being who you needed to be."

Holy shit. That hit me hard. I know I can be defensive at times, which I think comes from always having to defend my beloved state of New Jersey, or maybe from growing up playing on the street, where I learned how to be tough and keep a strong coat of armor around me.

5

READING

My evening ritual is pretty simple. I don't watch much TV and never have, but I do love getting into bed and curling up with a great book. Now, my puppy Paco lies on my chest while I read. My first love was fiction, but for these past two years I've been reading mostly the titles that I've recommended throughout this book. My mind and life were so scattered I couldn't concentrate on fiction, plus I was being turned on to so much great self-help and spiritual literature. I'm back now, though, reclaiming my love of reading fiction and enjoying it as much as ever.

So, between sleeping with my dog and writing in my journals, I'm turning into some new version of the cat lady. Who the hell will want to sleep with this nut? Truth be told, if I had some tall, dark-haired hunk of manhood lying next to me I probably wouldn't need to do any of this shit!

 EXPLORE

Daily Om
Madisyn Taylor

Hiring the Heavens
Jean Slatter

The Artist's Way
Julia Cameron

One Simple Thing:
A New Look at the
Science of Yoga
Eddie Stern

PLAYLIST | SUNSHINE

Changes
David Bowie

How Far I'll Go
Alessia Cara

Sunny
Bobby Hebb

I'll Follow the Sun
The Beatles

Sunshine on
My Shoulders
John Denver

A Place in the Sun
Stevie Wonder

Sunshine, Lollipops,
and Rainbows
Lesley Gore

You Can't
Hurry Love
The Supremes

All You Need
Is Love
The Beatles

L-O-V-E
Nat King Cole

California Sun
The Ramones

California
Dreamin'
The Mamas
and the Papas

Your Song
Rita Ora

Tubthumping
Chumbawamba

Shake It Off
Florence +
the Machine

Butterfly
Crazy Town

Woman's World
Cher

Sorry Not Sorry
Demi Lovato

Fight Song
Rachel Platten

Girl on Fire
Alicia Keys

Confident
Demi Lovato

Wings
Little Mix

Kings and Queens
Mat Kearney

I'm Coming Out
Diana Ross

Dogs Days Are Over
Florence +
The Machine

EPILOGUE

As I'm writing this last section of my book, I just realized that it's my one-year anniversary living in Southern California. The timing of this is not surprising to me because now I believe so much in a "blueprint" of one's life. Much like the snake shedding its skin, it is divine timing. I am where I am supposed to be at this moment.

I used to say to my girlfriends that I had a philosophy on the different chapters of life. The first chapter, between one and twenty-five years old, is when we are taken care of. We are granddaughters, daughters, nieces, sisters, and friends, but others are generally taking care of us. The next chapter, from twenty-six to fifty years old, we maybe get married and have children; we also likely have aging parents, so we are doing

"YOU CAN'T STOP THE WAVES BUT YOU CAN LEARN TO SURF."

the caretaking. My three sons know that I have often told them those were the happiest years of my life. But after that, from fifty-one and beyond, our children move out and then we are on our own; it's time to take care of ourselves. I know I personally struggle with

174

this because I'm a natural born nurturer and I'm not happy unless I'm taking care of others.

Life can be difficult. It is like an ocean with waves that ebb and flow. There are times when it is calm and other times when it is turbulent. The trick is to stay on your surfboard and ride the waves. The term "Hang 5" started here in California and represents your five toes hanging off the edge of the board. When my boys were teenagers, sometimes our relationship was tumultuous, and I'd tell my sister that I felt like I was on a surfboard holding on for dear life. I could see the shoreline, and I knew that if I stayed balanced and focused I could ride the wave of their adolescence until we all arrived safely to shore. An ocean is like a mother: she waits patiently as her charges go out to shore and return, she accepts the changes in the weather, and she welcomes all of the rivers that lead to her. I now find myself sitting on the sand—the ocean is literally out my kitchen window—and I feel so humbled as I look at its vastness. We can always use more humility. I know firsthand that the path I have been on these last few years has made me more humble, and I needed it. As I mentioned earlier, that change is difficult because we have to show a vulnerability, but being vulnerable makes us courageous. The thing I had to learn most was to be patient and to be okay with not knowing how it would end or where it would all lead. I'm still working hard on letting myself just go with the flow rather than controlling everything like I would have in the past. Now I try to respond rather than react. There were moments when I was paralyzed by fear, but I'm so proud of the courage I found and of the work I did to make changes in my life.

Looking back on notes from a conversation I had with Nicole here in Santa Monica in 2017, I was reminded that she kept saying to me, "You are at a rediscovery phase of your life. You are going through a metamorphosis and coming out of your cocoon. It is time to spread your wings like a butterfly." When reading about a butterfly's metamorphosis, I learned a lot. It's a very difficult and slow evolution, just like mine has been. I've had to learn to be patient and let the timing happen the way it is supposed to happen. Like the phases of metamorphosis, in life there are times when there is darkness before light. For instance, when a child is being born, they are happy in the embryonic sack, but when it's time for their birth they go from darkness to light, and it's startling and scary. That's why they cry when they feel air for the first time. I was basically in a bubble and did a karate kick with my very high-heeled shoes and popped the bubble. Imagine popping a bubble and suddenly swooshing out, inevitably landing on your ass. That's pretty much what I did!

Nicole also kept saying throughout our session how creative I was and how she saw a kind of *Eat, Pray, Love* book in me. Then, when I said I was visiting from Boston, she said, "I could have sworn you were a California girl!" So, I guess as I'm writing this epilogue, it's fascinating to be reminded of all of the changes that have happened and of the wonderful people I have met along the way. It's been truly difficult at times, like during the caterpillar phases, but I'm so grateful to my army of angels and to my army of family and friends who were there for me every step of the way. I feel so grateful for all that I've learned and for all of the incredible people I've met. I'm beyond blessed with so many supportive, caring, and kind family members and friends. I was surrounded by love as I explored new things, some of which have become essential threads in the tapestry of my life. I'm not sure I would have gotten through it without them.

I was introduced to my soul during this rediscovery phase as well. In the book *Seat of the Soul* by Gary Zukov, he talks about lessons for the soul to learn and how souls are seeking to heal. Every experience and every interaction we have helps us to see our soul. I never thought about my soul before this, but now I think about her while making decisions. I find myself thinking about her past lives and what she may be here in this lifetime to learn. I know one thing for certain: she needs to be in nature. I actually feel her happiness when I am walking in a field of grass or climbing a mountain. It's a lightness inside of me. And I know that when she's happy, I'm happy.

I will live my life going forward incorporating the many new things I explored, understanding that there really is no destination. The journey is the destination, and what a journey it has been. I will continue to learn and to grow because that is what keeps me healthy in mind, body, and spirit.

The four simple truths that I learned from the Vedanta Society will guide me throughout my life. These truly resonate with me and enable me to create good Karma. I will continue to do good and spread kindness. I will always love and respect God and be grateful all the days of my life.

I continue to be grateful for the life I have created for myself. As I read over my journals from these past few years, I get sentimental. I experienced sheer terror of the unknown, tearful moments knowing I had to close doors, and yet there was laughter with friends and excitement in learning so many new things. I really packed it in!

I hope you enjoyed sharing and reading about my transformation as much as I enjoyed experiencing and writing about it. I also hope you were exposed to some new areas that you would like to explore. Read, get a tarot reading, watch movies, have your charts read, journal, get out in nature, try something new that challenges you, and most of all, love—love yourself, love the people around you, and remember: the only thing that is permanent in life is impermanence.

GRATITUDE

I especially need to thank my best friend Lydia who called, emailed, or texted me every single morning. I love you with every breath I take.

For Karen, my other best friend, who I'm pretty sure was a sister or a mother from another lifetime. I'm lucky to have you in this life.

For my army of angels, who I prayed to every single morning and every single night, who brought me solace, and who gave me strength to make all of the bold moves I made.

My three sons and their partners who, throughout this difficult time, realized that our family could not only withstand this journey but prevail. Gregory was always there for me when I had strong physical reactions to all of the stress in my life.

My siblings Kitten, Hellie, Cassie, and my little brother Jason who were there for me every step of the way. I thought Jason would be helpful for my financial stuff but he was there in so many other ways. I loved how he and Shawn always would give me his kids' sports schedules so that I could attend their games.

My big brother Johnnie who was constantly saying, "Magoo, move to California!" Another thing he kept saying to me was, "Magoo, you need a puppy. You always loved the family dogs." He would take me to the movies and we'd talk about it over dinner afterwards. One night I said to our bartender, "If he wasn't my brother, I'd marry him!"

My mother was a good role model. When their marriage ended, she packed one suitcase and flew to California. As Dolly Parton once said, "If you don't like the road you're walking on, start paving another one."

Sheena, my Indian Goddess, who taught me a new way of eating healthy and helped guide me through meditations that really calmed me. I felt so nurtured. She also pushed me (gently) to write this book.

Andy would always, for some freakish reason, know when to check on me. I used to say it was like he was taking my pulse. I loved that I could talk to him about Qigong and all of the other things I experimented with this year.

Beverly, my Qigong master, who awakened me, Tarot Card readers who spooked me, and psychologists who tried their best to help me. Frank, who poked needles in me and made me take vitamins even though I complained a lot, and his wife, Sanda, who helped me turn a corner.

All of my girlfriends who I got shitfaced and laughed my ass off with! As I always say, "#luckygirl".

There were times I felt like a female Humpty Dumpty. Remember the nursery rhyme:

Humpty Dumpty sat on a wall
Humpy Dumpty had a great fall

All the King's horses and all the King's men
Couldn't put Humpty Dumpty together again

I picture a female egg carrying a pocketbook and wearing heels, walking along the edge of a brick wall when she falls and shatters into little pieces on the sidewalk. Only in my fairy tale, it's not the King's men but all of my friends who scurry around to gather the pieces and, like little Martha Stewarts, glue gun me back together again.

I'm grateful to my editor, who I enjoyed meeting each Monday over turmeric lattes in West Hollywood, and for the guidance he provided to me. He tried his best to keep it clean, but you know the saying: "You can take the girl out of Jersey, but you can't take the Jersey out of the girl!"

And, of course, my puppy PACO. He and his four siblings were rescued from a bad life situation in Tijuana, but I'm certain that he rescued me!

"Do one thing every day that scares you."

Eleanor Roosevelt

ABOUT THE AUTHOR

Megan Silletti O'Block was born in Hoboken, New Jersey, raised her three sons in Boston, Massachusetts, and now lives in Santa Monica, California. She enjoys long walks on the beach and hiking in the canyons of California with her rescue dog Paco. In the last few years, she has explored many new approaches to having a healthy, mind, body, and spirit. Through her travels around the world, she enjoys learning about different cultures and especially their cooking techniques. She loves entertaining and experimenting with herbs and spices that she didn't grow up eating. Two of her cookbooks that are available on Amazon are *Cooking for My Three Sons* and *Heart to Table*.